Developing

SUCCESSFUL BUSINESS LEADERS:

Exploring Past Encounters and Events that Help Define the Qualities Required of Successful Business Leaders

By Robert H. Smith

TABLE OF CONTENTS

INTRODUCTION

According to Amazon there are 34,600 books currently available discussing the many aspects of both leadership and management. This does not include the many thousands of articles and periodicals on the subjects written and disseminated each year plus the training offered by hundreds of schools, colleges, and universities. Moreover, it has been noted that up to $14 billion is spent each year on executive level management and leadership development.

The earliest references describing preferred management focus and leadership qualities have been traced back to the early Greek classics, of the fourth and fifth centuries B.C.. In the years since this early beginning, the discussion and depth of understanding of the individual qualities necessary for better leadership and management focus have grown exponentially. Today, the plethora of information and thought available goes well beyond the early history of discussion. Nevertheless, several of the concepts and ideas regarding management focus and leadership qualities remain unchanged.

Many of the current written references to understanding and definition are worthy of review, yet much of the work is primarily based on the theoretical thinking of consultants and educators and not based on any real-world experience. Some of the writings currently available offer questionable and confusing conclusions in today's fast changing contemporary environment.

The thousands of available books and articles on the subject cover almost every aspect of understanding, developing, or improving management and leadership qualities. It's nearly impossible not to find an element or aspect of leadership or management that hasn't been fully covered or discussed. Notwithstanding the multiple references to the rights, wrongs, goods and bad, do's and don'ts of these subjects, there seem to be only a limited number of experienced practitioners who have attempted to convert their everyday experiences to real-world lessons on the qualities necessary to exercise effective leadership and management.

The forty-two stories included in this writing are experiences extracted from an eventful period of banking in prior decades, yet the lessons from these events seem to remain universal in today's business environment. Additionally, the leadership qualities identified are common to any business experience, not just those found in the world of banking, finance, or the nation's largest companies. The experiences noted are drawn from a complex, regulated global environment; yet, the lessons are common to all businesses. There is something to be gained from each story by almost all business persons. In addition, the sequence of the stories offer a unique and challenging vision of a very complex period in business.

This book avoids theoretical assumptions in defining both leadership qualities and the broader core management focus. It is my hope that the preferred leader profile, desirable personal behavioral and value characteristics, and necessary operational skills identified as essential leadership qualities, can serve as an effective and meaningful beacon for new world business leaders.

Since the book discusses both management and leadership issues, it is important to understand how matters of both leadership and management are related. A successful business head needs to be both a strong leader and effective business manager in moving the entire entity toward a common vision of success. Strong and effective business leadership is about exercising the personal and group qualities that lead people to understand and believe in a common vision and collectively work toward achieving that goal. Managing is more about administering and making sure the broader responsibilities of the leader are being fulfilled.

CORE MANAGEMENT RESPONSBILITIES

Effective business leaders require a broad group of core management responsibilities in order to effectively and successfully operate their companies in fulfilling the needs of all those who have interest. The following are areas of management responsibility which should be continuously addressed as a principal focus of the leader's work.

A leader's core management responsibility is meeting the expectations of investor shareholders or owners of the company. While there are numerous areas of concern to the investors, their primary expectations are that the company is effectively managed so as to achieve the expectations for stock price or value appreciation. In addition, there is an expectation for dividend payments and earnings growth without assuming undue risk. The investor shareholders or owners also have expectations that the company's leadership will enhance the long-term potential and value of the company. It is critical for effective management that the leader is fully responsive and accountable to the owners or board of directors as representatives of the investor shareholders.

It is also essential to good management that the leader fulfills the expectations of employees at all levels. In order to maintain motivated, competent, productive staffing, leaders should meet reasonable employee expectations for fair compensation and a quality, safe, and opportunistic work environment.

In addition, strong management requires that leaders work closely with local, state, and national government entities and regulators to satisfy the expectations and needs of the community and its laws. This includes ensuring compliance with a multitude of regulations, plus satisfying reasonable quality and service expectations. This area of focus is necessary to gain support of all impacted parties in satisfying the strategic objectives of the company. All business decisions should consider fulfilling reasonable expectations of these groups as an essential element in meeting business goals.

The leader also needs to be responsive to meeting the needs and expectations of the customers. This includes offering quality products and services that fulfill business and personal needs consistent with satisfying the business strategies and return expectations of the company.

Lastly, there are several external affiliate groups that have a significant impact on selective aspects and elements of the business. Each affiliate group must be considered by the leader as an important management responsibility in achieving success. The affiliate groups that impact most all company include lawyers, accountants and their firms, the press, rating agencies, security analysts, as well as regulatory and government groups at all levels. The affiliate groups also include consultants and advisors of all types, local and national community groups, local and national industry groups, lobbyists, activists, unions, suppliers, third party contractors, joint venture partners, and in many cases the families of the company employees.

All affiliate groups are deserving of the individual and collective consideration of the leader and others within the company. Overall it is the leader's management responsibility to coordinate and balance all the interests and needs of those who impact and maintain an interest in the company.

PREFACE

After becoming the Chairman and CEO of the fifth largest bank in the United States in January 1990, I naively accepted the premise that my personal leadership and management acumen had been sufficiently honed and tested over nearly thirty years of banking leadership. I accepted the belief that I had the experience, knowledge, and qualities necessary to adequately deal with whatever issues might be confronted. As such, it seemed evident that the company's historical success and future aspirations could continue under my new leadership.

It was just a short period, however, before the complexities and challenges inherent in being the leader of 45,000 employees around the world and meeting the needs of five million customers became evident. The challenge also included meeting the expectation of 35,000 investor shareholders and managing the interests and impact of numerous affiliate groups that could influence our performance.

Until I was thrust into this new position, I did not recognize or consider the diversity and confluence of internal and external forces that could influence our performance and the personal skill set and qualities required to be successful as the leader of a major U.S. bank.

Prior to this new responsibility I had been successful as a junior leader and later as a more senior executive. During this period, I had relied on confidence in my personal acumen and gave limited consideration for structure or advice and guidance of those outside my inner circle. I had attended several external leadership and management programs to advance my thinking and qualities in order to become a more effective business leader and manager.

Until we faced our troubles, I was committed to independent and solitary thinking about our priorities and future aspirations. I looked to our bank's long history of successful performance and the ongoing acceptance of my style as I rose through the organization.

As I stepped forward as the new boss and during a short period preceding my appointment, I realized that many aspects of my view of good leadership and management were being challenged. I was struggling to consistently exercise well-received leadership and management practices. It was becoming evident that I must rethink and hone my capabilities by identifying and acquiescing to the necessary specific qualities required of successful business leaders.

If we were to succeed and as I was later to discover, even survive, it would be essential that the full team work in collaboration, each exercising strong leadership qualities, rather than follow independent paths. I had emerged from an independent free-thinking, unstructured business leader to one driven by the identification, execution and expression of several strong leadership qualities.

The experiences of this period were difficult and challenging. Yet the lessons learned from both successes and failures, clearly defined for the entire staff, the specific essential qualities necessary to effectively lead a company. The forty-two situations experienced are a few of the events that proved helpful in identifying the key leadership qualities required of successful business leaders.

The twenty specific qualities identified include important elements of a preferred leader's profile. These qualities also include a number of the desirable personal behavioral and specific value characteristics. Lastly, these qualities note several of the operational skills necessary to be a successful leader. Specifically, noted below, these qualities are described in more detail in the closing addendum and are offered for illustration throughout the stories.

PREFERRED LEADER PROFILE

- Possesses a strong understanding of financial issues (FINANCIAL UNDERSTANDING)

- Cognizant of how the economy impacts decisions (ECONOMIC KNOWLEDGE)

- Demonstrates a keen awareness of legal matters (LEGAL AWARENESS)

- Understands practices and business standards (UNDERSTAND PRACTICES AND STANDARDS

DESIRABLE PERSONAL BEHAVIOUAL CHARACTERISTICS

- Committed to the company (COMMITTED)

- Exhibits positive confidence (CONFIDENT)

- Acts decisively in resolving matters (DECISIVE)

- Undertakes action without fear (FEARLESS)

- Exercises a disciplined decision process (DISCIPLINED)

- Responds with patience (PATIENT)

SPECIFIC PERSONAL VALUE CHARACTERISTICS

- Exercises fairness in decision making (FAIR)

- Conveys compassion (COMPASSIONATE)

- Assumes accountability (ACCOUNTABLE)

- Acts with high ethical values (ETHICAL)

NECESSARY OPERATING SKILLS

- Effectively communicates with focused consistency (COMMUNICATIVE)
- Willing to listening and considering views pf others (COLLABORATIVE)
- Remains organized in addressing issues (ORGANIZED)
- Capable of determining and evaluating risk (PROTECTIVE)
- Skilled in developing opportunities and marketing strategies (CREATIVE)
- Effective in judging people (SELECTIVE)

NOTES TO THE READER

This book contains firsthand accounts of events that took place during my career in business. The events described rely heavily on my recollection of the times and events, personal notes, date books, and memoranda, as well as on broadly used and reviewed company publications, videos, audiotapes, annual reports, public filings, and securities analyst reports. The events also include information based on independent analysis, archival newspaper articles, consultants' reports, press materials, and public briefing information. To confirm some of the facts and numbers, or in limited cases where my recollection was foggy, I contacted the people involved to gain their independent recollection of particular events. In some instances, I have relied on secondary sources, including books, magazine articles, on-line databases, and impartial analysis to refresh my knowledge of the broader economic history of the time.

Where dialogue is used, it is accurate in fact and spirit to the best of my recollection. In the case of certain discussions, I have referred to notes I often kept of such events. Where appropriate, I have recreated dialogue by relying on notes and in some instances consolidated conversations and discussions that occurred over time. I have attempted to remain as faithful as possible to the information conveyed as well as the intent, flavor, mood, and attitude of the conversation and the verbal style of the people involved.

This book represents my independent views, thoughts, and interpretations of the facts, conversations, people, and individual feelings involved, all of which may or may not necessarily be universally shared by all participants. In some cases, I gained the assistance of Michael Crowley, a former writing associate, in conveying the meaning and spirit of the story.

To the best of my knowledge and belief, no information or data revealed in this book is considered classified, confidential, or secret within the context of the interests of Security Pacific, its subsidiaries, or their successors.

1

THE BEGINNING OF A TROUBLED ERA

CHARLES KEATING'S ADVENTURE

Enormous consequences are often the result of humble beginnings; a trickle begat the Grand Canyon. One impromptu meeting between a helpful bank executive and a soon to be disgraced real estate developer can set in motion the dynamics of a series of events that could lead to a near bank failure.

The banker was me, and my guest that day was Charles H. Keating, who years later would become the national image for the ultimate failure of the savings and loan industry. It was thirty-five years ago in April 1983, and I had no idea I'd just shaken hands with a human lightning rod. We sat down for a meeting that, had it not taken place, or had it ended differently, might have prevented the demise of my company, Security Pacific Bank, eight years later. I might also have saved the taxpayers $3.4 billion in cash required to bail out the Keating empire and the cost of numerous federal trials and appeals for fraud, racketeering, and conspiracy.

Charles Keating was a customer of ours, and that morning I'd received a phone call from one of my senior account officers. "Bob, this guy Keating wants to see you. Our loan experience with him has been great and he's become a real pioneer in real estate development. Will you talk to him?"

"What does he want?"

"He has expressed to me an interest in buying a California savings and loan."

Because we were one of Keating's primary banking relationships and we were active real estate lenders, it was only a minor surprise to me that a man who was one of the largest real estate developers in Arizona would express an urgent desire to see us. With $37 billion in assets, Security Pacific Bank was, in spring 1983, the second largest bank in California — smaller than Bank of America but larger than Wells Fargo and First Interstate banks — with more than 620 domestic and 36 foreign branches.

I thought for a minute, consulted my schedule, and said, "Yeah, send him up."

Keating was an impressive man: charismatic, knowledgeable, even elegant. He was six foot-five, with imposing teeth. His physique remained a testament to his youthful passion for swimming. It has been said, appropriately, that he had a "larger than life" quality about him. I offered him a seat.

"Mr. Keating, what is it you have in mind?"

As I expected, Keating was not at a loss for words. "I would like to buy a savings and loan."

I paused for a moment and asked the obvious question. "Why?"

He began by noting, quite rightly, that thrift institutions were having a rough time, and he saw it as an opportunity to buy into the savings and loan business. S&Ls were lenders to investors in real estate, he observed, and he was a real estate developer; it seemed like a perfect fit. If he could find the right S&L to buy, he saw considerable synergies. It could grow its deposit base, which would serve to finance various real estate projects that his other business interests developed.

While his objective made a certain amount of business sense, I cautioned him: "You know, Mr. Keating, the regulators aren't going to let you run a savings and loan like a captive finance company or a piggy bank. They're going to watch that pretty closely.

He knew all that and could deal with it, he said, and asked if I knew of any S&Ls in the West that were currently for sale.

"How much do you want to spend?"

"I'm thinking of maybe a $40 or $50 million investment."

"Well, as a matter of fact, I do know one institution." I could see Keating straighten up in his chair and begin to rivet his attention on me. This amount was perfect for acquiring a thrift I was thinking about.

The savings and loan I had in mind was called Lincoln Savings and Loan. Lincoln had the lowest ratio of delinquent mortgages of any thrift in the area, but like other Southern California thrifts, Lincoln was losing money because it was paying increasingly high interest rates to retain short-term deposits while continuing to earn low rates on its long-term fixed-rate home mortgages.

I knew Lincoln's number through a neighbor who had become a good friend of mine. Lincoln was an institution of about $1 billion in assets; this perfectly fit the amount Keating wanted to spend. Recently, my friend had mentioned that Lincoln might be sold, as they were uncertain about Lincoln and the S&L industries future.

Keating percolated. "I'm intrigued." He expressed an interest in further exploration of this "opportunity."

"I'd be happy to introduce you. However, we are in the investment banking business, and we'd like to represent you. I'd be happy to serve as an introduction, but I'd like you to go down and speak to my investment banking guy." I wanted Security Pacific to represent Keating, but I also wanted Security Pacific to get paid for it.

> *CREATIVE – Business leaders should continually seek additional business opportunities.*

> *COMMUNICATIVE – Business leaders should aggressively communicate to seek opportunities for new or expanded business relationships.*

"No problem," he said. "Set me up!"

Quickly, we drafted an agreement formally stating that Keating had hired us to represent and introduce him to Lincoln.

Keating was intelligent, but I could see he wanted to keep his cards close to his vest. He never tipped his hand in our early conversations that he might have more ambitious plans for Lincoln than just making home loans.

I phoned my friend at Lincoln and made formal arrangements for Keating's introduction. I accompanied Keating to Lincoln headquarters, where they had a short but productive conversation. Two weeks later, when Keating offered Lincoln $51 million—one and a half times its book value—they struck a deal. Keating quickly signed an agreement to purchase Lincoln Savings and Loan.

The expedited regulatory application was approved in early 1984. A few months later, when pressed, Keating told us he wouldn't pay us our contracted advisory fee of $250,000 because we "only" introduced him and didn't add much to the deal. After months of debate with his lawyers we ultimately settled with him for half the contracted fee. This was an interesting test of his character.

Seven months after Keating acquired Lincoln, I received a phone call from my friend there. "You ought to know that this guy Keating is not on the same course as everybody else. He's laid waste to top management, and the people Keating hasn't fired are going to walk. He's buying land in foreign countries, he's buying huge blocks of land all over Arizona. He's not making any real estate loans, he's making land investments and doing all sorts of strange things using the company deposits. So, as a friend I'm telling you to watch out."

I immediately talked with our credit people about this conversation. "The word I get is that this guy Keating is going off in all kinds of different directions, and we'd better watch out. Hopefully, now that he owns the S&L he won't need us anyway."

Mercifully, we did take this caution to heart. We stopped being Keating's principal bank.

PROTECTIVE – Leadership should identify situations, transactions, and relationships involving unacceptable risks and be willing to avoid those matters.

Home lending, as we recognized in the months that followed, was not Keating's objective. In 1984 Lincoln Savings and Loan granted only eleven home mortgages, four of them to employees. Keating was, to put it graciously, a man with bigger plans in mind.

While the regulators looked the other way, Keating promptly embarked on a series of "nontraditional" banking deals, carefully structured to capitalize on the newly established savings and loan rules and their liberal powers designed to keep the industry afloat. By the late 1980s, these deals triggered Lincoln's collapse and seizure by the government and Keating's personal fund-raising antics conducted through Lincoln began a long legal entanglement and ultimately a jail sentence.

Keating was certainly not the only fringe operator of the day. Michael Milken was known as the leveraged buy-out and junk bond king. He and other rogues of the period would become household names in the years ahead and were often heralded as icons and celebrities. This group perplexed and concerned me but somehow didn't change my often aggressive nature.

"WE DO DEALS"

On another later occasion in 1986, while flying from New York back to Los Angeles, I found myself sitting next to Abraham "Abe" Spiegel a man who made so much money in the stock market that he dropped out of school and became a stockbroker. With him on the plane was his son Thomas, the president and CEO of Columbia Savings and Loan. Tom along with Abe, his eighty-year-old father and my seat-mate, were the company's two leaders. Their current success accounted for Thomas's generous $9 million salary in 1985. The company was an enthusiastic buyer of junk bonds as one of a growing number of loyal disciples of Michael Milken. Thomas was said to so idolize Milken that he availed himself of every opportunity to display photographs of himself and Milken posing together at parties at expensive restaurants. A somewhat odd couple.

One third of Columbia's asset portfolio was junk bonds which served a contemporary vehicle and the key financing tool of leveraged buy-outs. Most of these high-risk, high-return junk bonds were initiated and distributed through Milken's Drexel Burnham operation..

I was surprised to find Spiegel on a plane like this, because it was common knowledge that they, in collaboration with Milken, had recently purchased a Gulfstream private jet. I introduced myself to Spiegel, who immediately figured he had a sympathetic listener beside him.

Columbia Savings and Loan had just gone public, and he and his son were on their way back to Los Angeles from New York. Soon after settling down, he began to gripe aloud to me. "I can't understand why we go public at such a low multiple to earnings. I can't believe we go to market at four multiples."

I finally took the bait. "Well, what kind of real estate loans do you make at Columbia?"

With obvious contempt for the naïveté of my question, he said with a strong accent, "We don't do real estate loans. We would never do real estate loans."

"Well, what do you do? I thought that was a core earnings generator of S&Ls."

"We do deals."

"What do you mean, you do 'deals'?"

"We do Biltmore Hotel. We do Newporter Hotel. We do junk bonds. Real estate loans are for fools. We can make more money doing deals."

I quickly determined that I did not want to do business with Columbia and did not solicit or make any arrangements for a further business contact.

PROTECTIVE – Leadership should be protective by avoiding business transactions that carry a risk level that exceeds the company's history, practices, and policies. In addition, effective business leadership should avoid business with companies or individuals that are considered high risk, unreliable, or unattractive.

DECISIVE - Business leaders should respond to matters decisively leaving no-doubt in the minds of their staff or customers as to the anticipated outcome or conclusion.

The following year I became aware that Columbia had purchased $3 billion in junk bonds, most of them through Milken. When a substantial portion of those bonds went into default the deals became imperiled and the Spiegel dynasty and Columbia S&L unraveled overnight. The company was taken over by the government in 1991.

KEATING WANTS MORE

In May 1988, five years after our first encounter, I received a call that chilled me to the bone. Keating said he had to come over and see me. Holy Christ, I thought, hadn't we finally gotten rid of him. What does he want with me?

I was, however, certain he wanted to borrow more money to shore up certain of his ventures undertaken outside of his Lincoln dealings.

When I revealed this to my marketing staff, they were strangely ecstatic because Keating was viewed on some fronts as a leader in the development of real estate projects. Obviously, a new generation of lenders was now working the real estate developer accounts.

"Whoa, whoa, whoa, hold on a second," I told them at the time. "This might not be the kind of guy we want to do business with. He is off on another planet. We gently dropped him from our principal customer list some years ago and his Lincoln S&L is in a lot of hot water."

"Well, he's back, they noted."

Since I generally met with anyone who wanted to see me, I set up an early morning appointment for the next day. Keating arrived with his entourage of five, which included his son, Lincoln's Chief Financial Officer, and a secretary, who was a real head-turner. Even before introductions could be made, the secretary jogged to the conference room phone, spoke for a few moments, rushed urgently to Keating, and whispered in his ear. Then she ran back to the phone, listened, returned to Keating, and whispered some more. For all I knew, she could have just been arranging a starting time for golf.

I waited patiently with a couple of my account officers while the antics continued for several minutes.

"Bob, what the hell is going on with Keating?" an early arriving account officer jokingly whispered in my ear, "he's either doing another deal or about to be indicted, I thought. But maybe it's just golf."

Finally, we began the meeting. Everyone took a seat, except for the secretary, who left the room, I supposed in search of more telephones.

"Charles, what brings you back?"

"Well, we'd like to rebuild our relationship with Security Pacific, and with yourself. After all, I was with you for a long time."

Oh my God, I thought. "To be honest with you, Charles, I haven't closely tracked your deals— (I almost said, 'crazy deals') very closely."

"Tell me a little bit about Lincoln. What are you guys up to? Are you making home mortgages?" A stupid, sarcastic question, I knew.

"Not so many of those. We're not really originating too many real estate loans. In fact, we don't even have a home loan department to speak of."

"How does Lincoln meet the S&L definition requirements? . . . How do you qualify as a savings and loan?"

"Well, you see, we buy mortgage-backed securities at the end of each quarter in order to comply."

"Charlie how then do you invest the deposit held at Lincoln to earn a return?"

"Well, we've bought land that we're developing, and we work with some of the key leveraged buyout (LBO) groups by participating in their junk bonds."

"So, you're taking a leveraged company and leveraging it even more by acquiring leveraged instruments?"

PROTECTIVE - Business leaders should identify matters that could expose their company at undo risk.

"That's a way of looking at it."

Jesus, I thought. "Charlie, I understand you've got a fortune tied up in an Arizona development called the Phoenician Hotel."

"Oh yeah, the Phoenician! It's going to be glorious! We've got $250 million in the Phoenician."

"I thought it cost more like $500 to $600 million."

"Well it did, but I've got a Kuwaiti Investment Company that's taken about half of it."

"Forgive me if I'm mistaken, but I thought that project was in big trouble."

"No, that silly business is all over with, thanks to the Kuwaiti's," he said.

"But from what I understand, it's costing more than $400,000 a room to build, and that means you're going to have to get significantly above market rates at 100% occupancy to get the cash flow.

I guess what I'm wondering is don't you think it's going to be somewhat difficult to find people willing to pay nearly double the best vacation rate available at other top Phoenix resorts?"

"Oh, don't worry. The Phoenician is absolutely going to work out fabulously. You come down there sometime and enjoy yourself. It will take your breath away."

His secretary, meanwhile, continued to hop back and forth like a cardinal dipping through a birdbath, in and out of the room, phone to phone, then back to Keating to whisper in his ear.

To get the meeting back on track, I asked him to give me some more details on the thrift's assets.

"What else are you doing, Charlie?"

"Oh, we're part of some of the LBOs with Sir James Goldsmith and some of the other guys. We've got Milken's Drexel deals. All the big boys are in the deal with us. By the way, have you heard about Rancho Vistoso?"

"No, I haven't. Fill me in."

"Well my God! A couple of wealthy partners and I are involved in this stupendous undertaking outside Tucson, a utopian dream community called Rancho Vistoso. We're going to build 11,000 homes on 7,430 acres of land. It's going to be something else. And then we're working on some real surprises."

"That sounds interesting and all, Charlie, but please understand that from our point of view, the types of assets you're discussing are not very liquid. A big part of Arizona is in severe economic trouble and has been for some time now and your projects are typically funded with shorter-term S&L deposits that might not renew if you get into trouble."

PROTECTIVE – Better business leaders should identify high risk situations.

ECONOMIC KNOWLEDGE – Business leaders should be cognizant of how the economy and economic trends can impact their actions.

"That's an exaggeration. Besides, it doesn't matter so much to us because these investments are geared toward doing business with the good long-term partners. We've got good deals."

"Be that as it may, you're creating long-term illiquid assets and not assets that have any liquidation value. Security Pacific would need to know, were we to loan you money, how we would get the money back when — or I should say, in the event that your primary source of repayment fails or is delayed. For example, if the deal stalls or doesn't make it for any reason, how do we get our money back?"

"Hey, you can always trust me. That shouldn't be a concern. My deals are all good deals, and they're going to be mesmerizing when they're finished, not to mention fabulously successful, and we really want to do business with you and your institution. I was with Security Pacific for a long, long time. And now you own the Arizona Bank right in my own backyard." Don't you really want to serve your good Arizona customers?"

"I know, Charlie. Let me think about it. But I doubt if we'll be interested," I said, knowing that my decision had already been made.

After the meeting, I conferred with my account officers. "What did I tell you? I wouldn't touch his deals with a ten-foot cattle prod."

Although it was fascinating to watch a man like Keating at work, I felt it would have been financial suicide to lend him money again.

DECISIVE – When the risk and exposure of a situation are beyond the company's standards and policies, business leaders should act decisively.

As the savings and loan industry collapsed costing owners several billion dollars, Keating and Lincoln as well as Columbia became part of this collapse. Keating, who was eventually convicted and sent to jail for a period of four and one-half years, became the "poster child" of this great financial failure and savings and loan industry collapse.

But near the end of the decade many banks, including our bank, had not seen the inherent risk of accelerated asset growth. We had also avoided the risks inherent in operating with very little capital or employing growth strategies based on leveraged financing.

These events and these characters set the tone for what was to come. A plethora of highly ambitious real estate developers moved much of their business from the collapsing free-wheeling S&Ls to banks. These real estate moguls, along with their banking partners, maintained a belief in an indestructible California economy. They also saw leverage as the God of growth and profits. They held a general misbelief that the government and the banking regulators were on their side working to assist in the success of the banking community. This was a set of grossly mistaken assumptions.

AUGUSTO PINOCHET TO THE RESCUE

Our aggressive nature with a focus on growth and leverage and our ambition to be among the top five banks in the United States had its beginning in the latter half of the 1970s. Fearing a Communist takeover of Mexico and Latin America during this period, President Ronald Reagan was politically supportive of those leaders in Central and South America who lead democratic regimes, or as an alternative were considered to be benevolent dictators. Augusto Pinochet, who had overthrown Chilean communist president Salvador Allende in a military coup during the early 1970s, was one of those leaders who gained support of the Reagan administration. Even though he was accused of significant human rights violations, Pinochet's staunch anti-communist stand permitted him to be cautiously supported by the U.S. administration.

In order to show continuing support for democratic as well as anticommunist regimes, the administration silently supported U.S. bank participation in development loans to Mexico and all the Central and South American countries. The loans undertaken by the banks were high return infrastructure loans that were funded by what was called petrol-dollars or funds deposited in U.S. banks by Middle-Eastern countries who were benefitting from rising oil prices. By 1983, $310 billion of loans had been pumped into these Latin American countries by the international banking community in support of the U.S. interests in promoting capitalism and keeping communist regimes out of the Americas. By the start of this period Security Pacific had a little over $4 billion in public and private sector loans outstanding to eleven Latin American countries.

Most of these loans were denominated in U.S. dollars and carried high rates of interest, with maturities ranging up to ten years. Because of poor economic conditions in these countries, including high levels of inflation, growing unemployment, declining currency values, and lost trade revenues, many of these loans were suddenly falling into default. Most of the countries could not accumulate enough U.S. dollars to even keep the interest current. By 1983, nearly all of the countries had failed to meet their obligations, resulting in a fairly universal declaration of default on the payment of both principal and interest. They noted that they had only limited sources for U.S. dollars, and in lieu of payment they requested bank concessions including extensions or renegotiation of the loans.

As a result, we were left with $4 billion of nonperforming loans without any certainty or plan for repayment. Recognizing the scope of the banking exposure and the potential losses, regulatory and Federal Reserve policy was adjusted to allow these loans to remain as assets on the balance sheet of the banks, reclassified as long-term workouts. We did not have to reserve or charge-off any amount, even though there was certainty that some portion or all the loans were uncollectable.

This Federal Reserve action established a precedent that under certain circumstances, larger banks would not be allowed to fail and their mistakes would be protected by the government. A few years later we mistakenly relied too much on what turned out to be this false assumption. In the next decade, we would discover that the government would not always be our friend and protector.

We remained positive, hoping to find workable alternatives or partial collectability from these countries. I was asked by the bank to aggressively identify optional forms of collection as a means of at least partial repayment. After several trips and meetings with the financial heads of most of these countries, I concluded that straight collection of either principal or interest in the near term of seven to ten years was not a possibility. We realized that we must look to more aggressive and perhaps creative strategies to get some of our money bank.

Pinochet's Chile was one of our debtors; they had borrowed a little over $200 million, all of which was now in default. As the country was aggressively seeking to privatize companies that had been taken over by the government following the coup and a deep recession, we conceptualized the exchange of their debt for participative ownership in these newly privatized companies. In other words, we would accept payment of the loans in pesos if we could invest those funds in major privatized Chilean companies and be allowed to sell those companies or withdraw income after a few years.

We had arranged to meet with the country's leader, Augusto Pinochet, in a private session to discuss the concept and then, hopefully, work out the details of an exchange with the country's finance minister. I wasn't sure whether this was a dream or a real option, but I felt we should give it a try. I also wasn't sure if this had ever been done or what the other banks were contemplating. The fact that it was likely that Pinochet had been previously briefed on the concept and at least agreed to meet gave me some hope. As we were driven to the Presidential Palace for our meeting, I tried to conceptualize what I should say and how I could gain acceptance of this bold concept. Perhaps gaining an interest in a bank or a utility or anything with a reasonable hard value and stability would be better than a loan in default.

CREATIVE – Business leader should seek solutions that are often outside normal methods or techniques in order to alleviate serious problems.

We entered the palace and were immediately subjected to a body and electronic search. My bodyguard, who was a little crazy, was able to slip a knife into a protected area after leaving his gun at the guard gate. We were placed in a private room to wait for the country's leader. After about thirty minutes, a military officer in full regalia entered saying the General would now see us. Pinochet had retained his military stature and rank following his coup some twelve years prior.

We were led into a large room that as we entered threw us into both sudden shock and fear. Apparently. Pinochet and his generals had decided to have our meeting on Chilean television and coming from a dark area, the lights in the room were enough to suggest we needed a cane or a seeing-eye dog. We were led to our seats in front of a raised platform where Pinochet sat in a large red chair, adorned in full military splendor with gold shoulder epaulettes his gold-laced military hat and enough chest medals to fill a grocery bag.

I was in a near panic, having been unaware of the television idea and seeing eight or ten other military personnel standing at Pinochet's side on the platform with what looked like AK-47s. I wondered if his air force might be in the other room. I knew that my bodyguard would look silly or be dead if he decided to pull out his knife. Unfortunately, other than asking about the swap concept, I had no other thoughts on my agenda.

"What do you want to talk about?" he opened the conversation without a handshake, a smile, or even a hello. He had limited English language skills and was able to understand more than he could speak.

I explained the idea of swapping the debt we held for assets, to which he immediately responded with a grin and nod. Through his translator, he said that it was an interesting idea and asked that I should talk and follow up with his finance minister, Mr. Bhute, that afternoon. It sounded like the idea had been preapproved as a workable concept.

"What else is on your mind?" he asked through his translator.

My God, I thought, what do I say? Perhaps, thank you and then give him a wave good-bye. No, I have to be a good guest and prolong this discussion a bit. Then a troubling thought went through my mind, and I spoke without much forethought.

"Yes," I said. "There is a deep concern on the part of many in the United States and members of our Board of Directors about the reported human rights violations and detained opposition groups in your country. Some reports even note deaths among your opponents. How can I assure my Board of Directors that this is not the case, and we should seriously consider owning assets in Chile?"

There was a deep pause, and I thought that I had just asked the wrong question and perhaps would be shot or placed in jail with his other opponents.

After a few moments he responded in a way that shocked me. "Mr. Smith, these reports are all false, made up, and reported by the New York Times, the Washington Post and Chicago Tribune based on information provided by the Russians and their Communist leaders. They are all lies, and I can prove it.

Certainly, short and to the point, I thought but not deserving of any response other than a thank-you and a nod. I am way over my head in this discussion, I thought, and hoped I could safely escape to meet with the finance minister that afternoon.

I wasn't sure what to expect next as I sat in Mr. Bhute's office later that afternoon. After about fifteen minutes a gentleman entered with long hair, a head band, chiseled body wearing short white pants with tennis shoes and high white socks. He looked just like Bjorn Borg the international tennis player. I wondered if we were going to have a game of tennis or talk about a swap. He introduced himself, but it seemed that this was his daily dress. He spoke good English and said he was trained and was a disciple of the Friedman economic principles taught during his time at the University of Chicago.

We discussed the exchange idea, which he noted would be helpful in the development of their new stock exchange and would assist in the development of capital to support their privatization strategy. For the $200 million they owed us he offered a small bank, 15% of a copper mining company, and 10% of a utility power company. We had no idea what each was worth, but we knew he had obviously thought through the transaction. We got some financial detail and told him we would examine the material and get back to him shortly.

There was little more we could know from the information provided other than it all seemed better than defaulted country loans without the possibility of collection in the near term. We did the deal.

CREATIVE – Business leaders should be willing to consider new ideas and concepts even though the risks are uncertain yet the risk of maitaining the status quo is also high.

Ultimately, our ownership of the copper company and utility were sold for over $300 million, and the bank, which we sold three years later for $50 million, currently has a market value capitalization of over $1 billion. As it turned out, we were negotiating blind, but were certainly lucky.

2

THE RULES CHANGE

A BAD CASE OF FIRREA

"When Congress implemented FIRREA, the man they most had in mind was Charles Keating."— Daniel Fischel, Payback.

In the wake of the Charles Keating disaster and meltdown of the S&Ls, the relationship between politicians and bankers became strained and precarious. Bankers were now personae non grata on Capitol Hill. Senators and Congress people did not want to be seen within a mile of a banker. They had been stung by the events surrounding the "Keating Five" in which this human lighting-rod had attempted to coerce the actions of five U.S. senators. And to prove that they meant it, in late 1989 Congress passed a draconian law called FIRREA: the Financial Institutions Reform, Recovery, and Enforcement Act. Generally described as "a call for prompt corrective action," it was in truth a law whose secret determination was to make sure that nothing like Keating's savings and loan flop ever recurred.

FIRREA was a lengthy and complex set of provisions whose full impact on banking and Security Pacific we hadn't yet fully discerned. All we knew was that FIRREA mandated sweeping changes in the examination, supervision, and disposal of insolvent thrifts. Incredibly, our early misperception was that FIRREA would be helpful to banks.

This distortion was based on tunnel vision: our attention to particularities within FIRREA to the exclusion of the larger picture. By accelerating the seizure and liquidation of ailing S&Ls, FIRREA did remove some competition and make it easy for banks to acquire defunct thrifts. Among the reasons for doing so was to "rescue" (i.e. hijack) an existing customer base and assume the deposits it represented. This was a rapid way to augment regional presence or solve a short-term funding problem.

In early 1990, shortly after the passage of FIRREA, Security Pacific acquired Gibraltar Savings and Loan to grow our deposit and customer base. But we didn't just buy Gibraltar; we bought it with impunity. And we gave the credit to FIRREA.

"Thank God for FIRREA," I told my staff. "FIRREA made this possible."

The Resolution Trust Corporation (RTC), a federal agency established under FIRREA, seized the failed Gibraltar bank with an intention to auction it to the highest bidder. At the close of the sale, the RTC would pay the acquiring bank to assume full responsibility for deposit liabilities, net of acquisition costs. Their process was to remove the assets, which were the loans. Later they planned to sell the loans on a discounted basis to cover some of the difference. The government would absorb the shortfall.

When I saw that Gibraltar was identified for sale, I concluded that we had to purchase it to remedy a very unusual funding situation. Security Pacific utilized short-term borrowing instruments to fund a large portion of the assets or loans of its bank and holding company subsidiaries. We had significantly overborrowed in the short term, using primarily commercial paper and interbank fed funds. This tactic was somewhat risky but advantageous to our banks as long as we were considered among the nation's premier financial institutions. We could benefit significantly from the interest rate arbitrage between lower short-term rates and higher long-term rates.

I felt, however, that overuse of the technique had put us in a tenuous position and put the bank at risk. The ratio of such funding when compared to the size of our institution, given the overall size of the market for short-term funds, exposed us to danger. At this moment, we had over $14 billion worth of short funding, composed of about $7 billion of commercial paper in the holding company and another $7 billion of fed fund or overnight interbank borrowings in the bank. I wanted to do something about this, and acquiring Gibraltar would be a quick $5 billion fix, at least for the bank.

PROTECTIVE – Business leaders are expected to identify any matter that can create unusual risk to the company

In emergency meetings I suggested we pursue Gibraltar. I felt the only quick and certain way to correct the funding exposure without compromising our short-term earnings was to purchase deposits. "Gibraltar," I pointed out, "is such a disaster that the RTC is selling it without any loans." I also mentioned that it was somewhat unusual to purchase a defunct thrift to access its deposits.

Our Chief Financial Officer or CFO thought Gibraltar was a can-do and a must-do. "Let's bid on it when it comes to the market."

We qualified and submitted our proposal. Our bid $144 million in cash, about 3.5% of deposits was our winning bid.

CREATIVE – Finding new ways to solve issues, finding new markets, expanding existing opportunities, or meeting structural needs are important abilities of strong business leaders.

Although we knew Gibraltar was a local S&L competitor with branch offices scattered in various parts of our market, we essentially bought it sight unseen, with the carefree tenacity of a child screaming for a particular toy at a garage sale.

We celebrated our acquisition. "The first thing we ought to do is send a telegram to Congress and thank them for FIRREA," I said, expressing an appreciation I would soon regret.

One of my staff noted that he believed FIRREA was the direct result of Keating. "You did it. You set up Keating, then he screwed up and got us FIRREA. You put a crash-test dummy in a Lincoln, he crashed the car, and we got FIRREA for better or worse."

The regulators had found their backs to the wall as, in hearing after hearing, Congress bludgeoned them with allegations of having looked the other way as the S&Ls fell. Congress was embarrassed and, in response, passed FIRREA to prevent this from ever happening again. The bank examiners were determined to broadly interpret and utilize its powers under this new law with the full force of their authority. The regulators had endured enough. Their implicit chant: "This S&L debacle will never happen again, you can believe that. If there is not full and strict compliance with our laws and oversight, heads will roll until the banking industry looks like a bowling alley during tournament week."

When FIRREA became law, the American Bankers Association was enormously pleased and regarded it as insightful legislation that was a triumph. FIRREA, as they understood it, focused aggressively on S&Ls, would curb the competitive threat they posed to banks, and appeared more or less to leave banks alone. But as we would soon find out the trouble was in the details. It wasn't only the thrifts who were to be affected by FIRREA.

As FIRREA and its regulations were published and made available to banks, it became evident that it encompassed several hundreds of pages of complex regulatory detail. When I examined an abridgment of FIRREA's key points, I was initially enthusiastic. It required S&Ls to adopt new capital standards. It transferred regulatory powers previously held by the Federal Home Loan Bank Board to a new agency called the Office of Thrift Supervision (OTS), under the auspices of the U.S. Treasury Department. It abolished the defunct Federal Savings and Loan Insurance Corporation to be replaced by the Federal Deposit Insurance Corporation. But there were more obscure points that were not highlighted. I didn't understand what it meant for the banks. I puzzled over the details with our Chief Legal Counsel.

"FIRREA? What does it really do to us?" I asked.

His eyes crinkled behind his glasses. "Its stated intention is clearly to reform the regulatory system and tighten restrictions on thrifts as well as banks, including us. As you can see, the act is very compendious. I haven't read the entire thing yet, but I know it comes down very, very hard on the S&Ls. It essentially puts them six-feet under"

Our Chief Legal Counsel had been with Security Pacific for nearly thirty- years. He was a man of supreme integrity. Unfortunately, he was also an unrelenting and chronic chain smoker, so much so that in the prior year he had to have a leg amputated because there was so much cardiovascular blockage. Even after that dire turn of events, he was unwilling or unable to kick the habit. Security Pacific had a "No Smoking" policy for everyone, or almost everyone: I'd modified it slightly, to read Absolutely No Smoking Anywhere Except for Specified Offices. He was a spectacularly bright and comprehensible attorney. If he couldn't solve a problem directly he knew how to find someone who could get it solved.

We were all getting impatient and pressed him. "But isn't it a good law for us?"

"Well," he said, "it's—I think it's a good law. It's enormously complex. I need to read it closely and sit down with our loan people to discern if and how it directly impacts banks. It facilitated our purchase of Gibraltar, didn't it?"

I shrugged my shoulders and tried to get him to disgorge whatever reservations might be in his mind. "It looks extremely thorough to me, for something created by Congress. Anything that cracks down on thrifts is good for us. Who can argue with the fundamental sanity of this law that reduces competition?"

"We'll see. Because of the bill's density and obscurity, it could take some time—perhaps months—to fully recognize its implications and impact on us."

"Make it weeks or even days," I said.

He hobbled back to his office for a cigarette.

Our ignorance and bliss about FIRREA was enjoyable while it lasted. When the reversal came, it was the shock of our lives — a direct hit, a missile fired directly up the bank's fanny. As I began to review new valuation reports on criticized real estate loans, I saw that something was dramatically different about the way in which the properties were being valued by appraisers, and then adjusted down by the regulator after discussions with the appraisers.

"You've got to figure this out," I told our CFO. "I mean, Holy Christ, I'm looking at a loan we made for $24 million that was secured by a piece of property appraised at $30 million a few months age. This report says it is now worth $18 million under the FIRREA appraisal standards. We're going to have to write this loan down another $8 million because we can't carry loans at values that exceed the underlying collateral. If FIRREA is already impacting appraisals, what is so darn hard about looking at that section for starters? This could be a big problem and it needs your attention, now."

"I understand that's a bunch of baloney. I'll get right on it," our CFO said.

"How can it be baloney when I'm seeing the results and writing down loans?"

COMMITTED – Business leaders should be intent on finding answers to issues that can seriously impact the future of the company

If it had only been a single write-down of $8 million on one particular loan or an aberration that would have been a tolerable inconvenience. But something was very wrong: every new appraisal reflected large reductions in valuation. Security Pacific had billions of dollars of such loans, many of them scheduled for reevaluation or reappraisal in the next twelve months.

PATIENT – The willingness of business leaders to seek issue resolution while remianing patient is important; however, it should not be used to rationalize the lack of attention or a commitment to timely issue resolution.

A week later, a flurry of new reports arrived. I read the new appraisal on a commercial land development that we had financed in Tampa, Florida. Good developer, good location, good project, perhaps a bit ahead of its time; but we still believed in the ability of this project to succeed. But for some reason the appraiser had assumed that it would require eighteen years for the project to be completely finished and occupied and he or she had discounted this slow build-out at a 15% annual rate, resulting in an $8 million current valuation on a development that cost $22 million and was appraised at $26 million just two years before.

I pressed harder and harder for answers. "This is unbelievable. What the hell is going on here and how does everyone else seem to understand the changes mandated by FIRREA and we don't. Will someone just read the frigging thing and tell me what it says. I don't think that is so difficult."

"We're trying to get our hands around this thing. I'll get back to you as soon as I find out," our Chief Credit Officer or CCO said.

The next day I popped into our CFO's office.

His lair was a monument to one brilliant man's productivity, and he often labored into the late night, only to emerge from the office after arriving at dawn with a precious menagerie of financial updates and the befuddled countenance of Tor Johnson wandering through a graveyard in Plan 9 From Outer Space. Hopelessly cluttered, his office looked like World's End.

He was a man who was mesmerized by numbers, collected stacks of paper like a recluse spider, and had no idea how to organize an executive office. I had difficulty finding him amid the stacks. In fact, the office was such a catastrophe that we had to film his portion of the quarterly video report to shareholders in a specially devised "set" designed to look like a respectable CFO's office.

I found our major staff executives in our CFO's offices looking unusually grim. No smiles. "Say, guys, what exactly is going on with the appraisals? Can't you all find out? Call someone, the ABA or Bank of America, but get the answer." I was trying to stay calm but was now getting totally pissed.

I was very upset as new appraisal reports now inundated me; the situation was serious, it was out of control.

There was a $30 million property being developed by a large California developer that had been revalued at $24 million. Security Pacific had pumped $54 million into a project called Dove Canyon. Its prior valuation at $70 million had been reappraised to $44 million. A $215 million property had been valued at 60% of its previous value. The Sir Francis Drake Hotel, whose value we believed to be $46 million, had been revalued at $33 million. The Northtown Mall, which had been initially appraised at $128 million, had been reappraised at $98 million. A hotel operation in Philadelphia formerly valued at $21 million was now worth $7.8 million. In every instance Security Pacific faced the imminent write-off of millions of dollars. It just went on and on, without explanation.

Hearing me enter, they all looked up. "We've found out what's going on," our Chief Legal Counsel said after my opening harsh comment. Looking a bit ashen, he put out a cigarette with one hand while in his other hand he had a Xerox copy of a legal document. "We found it! In order to get a handle on this you've got to understand this innocuous provision of FIRREA. Buckle your seatbelt."

"I'm buckled," I said, bracing myself.

"I'm looking at it right here," he announced in exacting, lawyer-like enunciation. "12CFR34, subsection C, Appraisal, Title 11 of FIRREA directs the appraisal of all real estate collateral be made to represent a cash sale, solely on the basis of what the entire property would sell for within the next twelve months to one buyer. The valuation can't consider financed sales, split property sales, or multiple buyers."

"That's bull," I said.

"No, it's true. It no longer matters what we think land could be worth in the future. In addition, it stipulates that all outstanding real estate land development and mini-perm loans will also have to be reappraised to current value. This means all appraisals will essentially be made as if it were a fire sale. This includes performing loans whose terms are modified, even with a slight variation in timing, lease terms, or use."

"No way. Some of these properties, we know, will always be worth a great deal. And what took you so long to find this out? How can I get finished appraisal reports without you knowing why it's done a certain way?"

Without immediately answering that question the CCO sadly shook his head. "It doesn't matter what we anticipate for the property; it must be appraised on the basis of what it is worth today. In other words, if we have even small problems with a real estate loan, we have to deal on an 'as is' valuation. No long-term solution. All valuations must be made based on what the whole property would fetch from a single buyer within twelve months."

"But, but—" I stammered. "We made loans based on what land or development would be worth over the time its developed in a stabilized economy.

"That's the nut of the problem. The figures that you've seen and trouble you've identified reflect that disparity."

"But we're talking about millions—perhaps billions—of dollars in valuation differences."

"I suspect we are talking about billions of dollars," our CCO added; he had turned a chalky white. "It's not a good thing for us. Also, in response to your question, and even though it would not have really mattered, we should all have known this earlier. We should have been advised of this when the bill was being drafted."

This was an understatement. Our bank was dependent on real estate to a degree that was frightening and had been since 1932 when our predecessors christened a new Real Estate Division. Despite the Great Depression, real estate was considered a necessary and prudent investment for a bank that proclaimed its economic roots to be the California land itself. We were committed to the land, and we never looked back. The notion that loans on real estate might become the weak link in our balance sheet in light of no historical antecedents whatsoever was unthinkable. It never occurred to us that there could be a prolonged and very serious economic downturn in our home state of California, or that legislation as ghastly as FIRREA— seemingly engineered to sink our bank, would come our way.

Our Age of Innocence had promptly given way to the Age of Panic.

I did not take this revelation well. In fact, I was severely shaken. "What are they trying to do to us? Congress and the regulators don't know what the hell they're doing. Just because the S&Ls attracted a bunch of crooks doesn't mean they have to penalize the commercial banks. This is no small thing! Security Pacific is somewhat unusual in that we have more money in real estate development than most other banks, particularly here in California, and our economy is showing many signs of worsening. We're into real estate up to our necks."

I knew that our real estate portfolio was going to be very hard hit. If we suffered any further economic downturn, we were not as well prepared as a lot of other banks to handle it; we had only a minimal capital level, we were over short-funded, and I believed we were in very serious trouble.

"Good God," I said, "This is no joke. Jesus, the bank could fail over this kind of change."

Over the following weeks the news of subsection C spread like wildfire among our top management.

"What's going on?" our tech leader asked. You could hear a pin drop as I began a staff meeting.

"It's FIRREA," I replied.

"FIRREA hurts us? I thought FIRREA was a victory. The ABA called it a triumph."

"FIRREA is no triumph. It's a piece of you know what." Absolutely killer legislation."

"I'd like to read it myself."

"It's buried in here." I showed him the provision.

He read it slowly. "What does this mean for Security Pacific?"

"It means we're in the toilet— that's what it means. If a loan gets into trouble or the terms aren't met on time, we have to write it down — now."

"The government got us into this mess, they have us by the balls," he said, "but they should help get us out."

No, I thought. That was always the hope, but seldom the reality. What the government excelled at was getting banks in trouble and leaving them to twist in the wind. All that will be left is the crumbs off the king's table.

"How much exposure do we have out there?" he asked as the rest of the group listened intently. "How much is subject to a write-down?"

"Simply put, of our $70 billion total loan portfolio, $13.5 billion are real estate land and development loans and about $4 billion are mini-perms or five to ten-year non-amortized loans on mini-malls, apartments and other developed real estate. Most of these are totally dependent on the project cash-flow for debt service. We also have about $4 billion of unfunded real estate commitments and standby letters of credit," our CCO explained.

"If these numbers are right," I added, "our real estate loan exposure is over 20% of our total loan portfolio. That's $17.5 billion of exposure, excluding the commitments, subject to this new valuation methodology." I looked at our tech guru, "That's why FIRREA could be a disaster for us. This is ugly. Congress has just handed us a pistol in which every chamber is loaded, told us to put it to our head and take our chances by pulling the trigger."

I jotted down some calculations on a notepad. "If these appraisals continue to reflect this trend, there will be about a 30% valuation discount on a $17.5 billion real estate portfolio. In this case we would have to eat over $5 billion and that is more than our capital. We would lose everything, God damn it. Am I overstating it, or are we screwed?"

"No," our CCO said, "I agree that is a quick. Simple, yet accurate analysis."

The fact of the matter was that FIRREA was a catastrophe, and its malignant effect on our real estate loan portfolio could not possibly be overstated. Worse, if it was true that the legislators who penned FIRREA did so with Keating specifically in mind, I was now fully cognizant of the fact that I was the unwitting accomplice and coauthor of the pernicious law that would cripple our bank irrevocably.

3

THE OUTLOOK TURNS DARK

GETTING INSIDE THE STAGECOACH

By late summer 1990 with more and more dramatically lower real estate appraisals and loan write-offs plus growing economic weaknesses, I realized that our capital and perhaps our bank was seriously threatened. I was reasonably sure that these conditions would necessitate forced regulatory actions to supplement our capital position and other demands and restrictive steps, which are never attractive during troubled times. I realized that I had to find a solution to this possibility before our bank found itself in the regulatory penalty box, perhaps even becoming the FIRREA poster child.

We had for years danced with Wells Fargo about joining our two banks, having last discussed that possibility only a year earlier. While Wells had some of the same difficulties as ours, their capital position was much greater, and their portfolio of somewhat toxic real estate land and development loans was much less than ours. As the result of needing a quick permanent solution to our problems, I put in a call to Carl Reichardt, Wells Fargo's CEO, to once again explore the possibilities of a merger. He sounded very interested and we scheduled an initial private meeting.

Carl was a seasoned, respected banking leader who had built Wells Fargo Bank from a minor banking player to one of the four California major banks. He employed simple, basic strategies that were disciplined and effective. He never strayed away from what he knew, understood, and was in his space. He was reluctant to expand into any activity outside of the United States or any area that he didn't or couldn't understand. He made decisions based primarily on creating safe long-term value for his share-holders. He was so respected for his leadership and results that Warren Buffet and his companies had begun investing in the company and now held over 10% of the Wells Fargo shares.

We began meeting in August 1990 to seriously consider if we could find an acceptable arrangement to merge our two banks. We both knew that the benefits of consolidation with combined greater market presence and consolidated expense savings would add significant value to both our bank stocks.

During the first few weeks, I met with Carl approximately half a dozen times in San Francisco. During these excursions, I had routinely made the trips as low-key as possible. Most of these visits were made on the pretext of either meeting with customers or visiting with officials at the Federal Reserve. Banking journalists and analysts swarmed these streets and virtually all of them knew me. If even one of them suspected that I was meeting secretly with Wells — especially with this kind of frequency and under assumed names at hotels — it would be headline news that we were contemplating a merger.

During an afternoon in mid-September, on my way to actually meet with the Federal Reserve following a meeting with Carl, I was approached from behind by Sam Zuckerman. Sam was a well-known chromogen reporter for the American Banker whose primary assignment was tracking and reporting on the California banks. Sam was aggressive, snoopy, and generally annoying.

"How's it going, Bob?"

"Very well," I stuttered.

"What are you doing up here?" A deceptively simple question which, uttered in this particular cadence, indicated to me that this reporter was looking for a story. Perhaps any indication of secret, suspicious meetings or gatherings.

I swallowed hard with a lump in my throat. "Just up for a routine visit with the Fed."

"Another meeting with the Fed? I believe I saw you up here last week? And, I could have sworn I also saw you the week before that. Anything big brewing?"

"Have you seen your other banking counterparts recently? The California economy continues to cause trouble, doesn't it?" he continued, offering a staccato of questions, looking for something to open me up to a response.

"I see the Wells and Bank of America guys all the time. We're all tough competitors but we all want to see the California economy improve. We're trying to see if there is any effort we can take with the Governor or in Washington to improve this situation," I've got to run now so I'm a bit late," I said abruptly, as I propelled myself into the Fed building. Zuckerman looked startled by my rush of anxiety, but fortunately did not inquire as to why I was so uncharacteristically peremptory or why I was visiting the Fed without any of my colleagues.

> COMMUNICATIVE – *Business leaders should be open, honest, and ethical in response to questioning. This, however, does not mandate that answers are fully revealing, straightforward, or without disguise when other purposes or issues are more relevant to the mission of the company.*

My intent was to be as inherently ethical, honest, and truthful as possible, but the slightest revelation or hint of two big banks discussing a merger would have been big news to all involved in the banking community. Such openness could also have a significant impact on any deal, its terms and stock price, not to mention the employees and customers. It was not in our best interest to expose or hint at what was really going on in our ongoing discussions with Wells Fargo. As a result, I decided to be mostly noncommunicative both in Los Angeles and San Francisco about any other meetings and discussions that were underway.

> ETHICAL – *It is important that business leaders are capable of responding truthfully without revealing information that could prove averse to the broader interests of the company.*

As Carl and I continued to make progress in our discussions, we agreed to employ a third-party consultant in an effort to move our negotiations forward, memorialize our conclusions in written form, ensure follow-up, and track open issues.

Negotiations took off. The more we met, the more we agreed. And the more we agreed, the closer we were to a written agreement to merge. We fixed the exchange rate based on our most recent stock prices. The benefit ran equally to both companies and their investors and shareholders. We formulated what was nearly a workable complete plan. We determined that the consolidation offered unquestioned strength and unprecedented levels of economization and expense cuts. We decided that Wells Fargo would be the name of the company, and we discussed our respective executive roles. He would be the CEO, and I would be the COO. We were nearly in full agreement with an effort driven by mutual understanding and desire to see both our stocks rise. Within these discussions, I really wanted to benefit from Wells Fargo's stronger capital position and avoid the anticipated regulatory demands, yet we never discussed, and I did not point out the negative implications for Security Pacific of not reaching a final merger agreement.

The essence of the success we found in our discussions were based upon finding compromise and collaboration in resolving numerous issues. We were both listening and looking for common ground. We found that the potential of the final joining of our companies outweighed any other debatable issues. This work was before the collaborative idea of modern business dealing became the standard. Working cooperatively together was our mutual preferred approach to issue resolution and building a consensus.

COLLABORATIVE – Business leaders should seek a strong collaborative spirit that bonds the thinking of the participants for the best collective results. Thinking as a group and listening and compromising with the group participants has shown to offer the best results in achieving successful decisions.

We were exuberant; we had outlines, procedural manuals, organizational charts, business strategies, and five-year projections. I began to consult with our outside investment bankers and attorneys on the mechanics of the transaction. We told people about the plan only on a need-to-know basis.

By late November, everything was falling into place. The planets were in alignment. We had both spoken to our respective executive committees and boards and had obtained their support for this historic transaction. What a major event in the history of California banking, I thought, and it's really going to happen. We were so enthusiastic that we set a tentative date to get formal board approvals.

"I think we should wind this up with a written agreement and announce the deal in the second week of January, right after the holidays," Carl noted.

"That's a perfect time frame," I agreed. "We'll get the year-end pageantry out of the way."

"In tying up the loose ends, however, there are certain aspects of your bank that I need to understand better," he said.

"No problem, tell me what you need, and I'll get it for you." I was confident that there was nothing we hadn't yet discussed or that he didn't fully understand and accept.

The following day, they requested more complete and somewhat highly specific information about selected businesses and subsidiaries. I wanted to obtain the information without arousing a lot of suspicion from the involved staff. Of all the requested data I was most concerned about details of our swaps operation. This was a complex area that involved arranging the exchange of different foreign currency and interest rate obligations in equal amounts and within similar time periods. Swaps, in more complex arrangements, become derivative transactions. We operated one of the largest "swap books" in the world at that time. This operation had garnered a streak of accolades and a lot of publicity and media attention and was extremely profitable. But Carl wanted to know very specific information about our "swaps book" so that his people could assess its risk.

The trouble was that the swaps operation was decentralized, with offices located in several key financial centers, and it did not share the technological loop with the rest of the banking operations. Much of the documentation was in the United Kingdom and New York City. It was particularly hard to obtain swaps information without affecting or inflaming the paranoia of many people; to seek this kind of documentation was practically an admission that a drastic undertaking was in the works. My attempt to do so would look exactly like what it was — a sneaky type of due diligence — and would invariably set off warning alarms throughout the company.

For these reasons, I had no luck producing the full scope of information they had requested in exactly the configuration they had described.

PATIENT – It is important for business leaders to be calm and react to the situation with reason, remaining patient. An impatient reaction or response generally results in poor or irrational decisions and tends to create a higher level of risk to the company.

Towards the end of November, I convened my staff for an inventory of our loan portfolio and available reserves. Following the review, we arrived at the unsettling conclusion that, pending further analysis, we would most likely have to set aside substantially greater loan reserves than we had originally planned for the fourth quarter. If this augmentation was deemed imperative, I would have an obligation to announce both the decision to increase our loan loss reserve and the dollar amount to the public immediately.

The timing was awful. If required to make this public exposure, I would arouse enormous industry speculation and set off warning bells and cries of doom. It would be patently obvious to the press and analysts that this was not business-as-usual and that we were going to have a very poor year with a weak forecast for the year to follow.

The first week of December was a pivotal one. We had yet to decide absolutely on the necessity and size of the special addition to be added to the loan loss reserve. We had to make the decision soon after putting together the last bit of data and then publicly announce the decision promptly.

Carl and I met early that week to hopefully finalize our plans. At the same time, I had produced what I could in the way of information regarding the swap's operation. They said it was not quite what they wanted. The truth is that both Carl and I had some difficulty deciphering the information because neither of us understood the finer points of swaps ourselves.

We decided that our respective Chief Financial Officers should get together and attempt to reconcile whatever issues needed to be resolved.

As part of our discussions that week, I also reluctantly informed Carl that I was considering the need to make and announce an addition to the loan loss reserve and that action would most likely result in reporting a quarterly loss. Fortunately, this didn't appear to faze him as he continued to express enthusiasm for the merger, noting that it was already their expectation that we would have to supplement our credit reserves.

Then, toward the end of our optimistic face-to-face meeting in San Francisco, I was interrupted by his assistant who said I had an urgent call from my Chief Financial Officer.

"We've got a big problem," he said, showing considerable anxiety in his voice.

"What's the problem?"

"We had originally planned to issue debt securities this morning and, as you know, we can't do that with the reserve matter and a possible merger pending."

"Oh, hell. Well, what happened?"

My CFO, normally cool, calm, and reserved, now sounded close to panic. "Damned if I know! Knowing full well you were in discussions with Wells about a potential merger and that we might have to announce a special addition to our loan loss reserve, I told our guys to stop issuing securities in the near term. Obviously, somebody didn't get the word or didn't understand the directive. Here we have all these pending disclosures and they went ahead and issued debt in the public market anyway."

My mouth went dry as sandstone. I immediately knew he was right. We both knew it was a violation of securities law to embark on any public offering while important announcements of a material magnitude were pending.

I told him I would call back and set the phone down in its cradle.

"Is everything all right?" Carl asked.

FEARLESS – It is important for business leaders to remain calm and fearless under all conditions and circumstances. Reacting to difficult situations with extreme emotions or evidence of fear permits others to doubt the truthfulness, sincerity, and commitment of the leadership.

This was the biggest screw-up I could imagine. And the timing was the worst possible masterpiece of tragicomedy. Here I was, as deep as I could possibly be into negotiations with someone who I didn't want to look like a fool in front of, and I was mere hours away from pulling the trigger announcing an extraordinary charge to the loan loss reserve. I knew that the last place in this world we should be right now is out in the market issuing securities.

I was pissed off and embarrassed but knew that it was imperative that I remain calm and process this matter with patient and reasoned thinking if I were to successfully work out of this situation. But I was self-aware that in these important areas I was failing miserably. I was anxious and scared.

I solemnly briefed Carl on the problem. "I apologize, but I have to get back to Los Angeles. I will call you when I know more." I felt like I'd shown up for my prom date with my shirttail or perhaps my thing hanging out of my fly.

I hustled back to Los Angeles, where we I gathered with our Chief Financial Officer and attorneys.

I was nearly livid. "I don't understand how this could happen."

My CFO shook his head. "I told them not to."

"But it happened." At this point I didn't care who was at fault. I wasn't going to shoot anybody over it because I had so many other problems. First let's fix it I thought, and then I'll fire the morons.

I pointed out how inept we would look having to pull the offering. "We are really parading our ineptitude to the world. It demonstrates a lack of leadership and management control. I mean, it just isn't done."

My CFO noted that there was no choice. "We have to withdraw the offering of these securities right away."

While this was a very tough decision, I immediately gave the go ahead.

ACCOUNTABLE – Business leaders should assume full accountability for the actions or results of the company without considering the level of direct personal involvement in the decisions or actions.

DECISIVE – Once all the facts have been gathered and options considered, it is important for business leaders to act decisively and with unwavering conviction and confidence. Delaying or belaboring decisions only conveys weakness in the leadership and causes uncertainty in the minds of the staff.

On Thursday morning, December 6, as discreetly as such a clumsy thing can be done, we pulled the issue. As anticipated, warning bells sounded up and down Wall Street. Reuters, AP, Business Wire, the Wall Street Journal, American Banker, and a myriad of reporters and analysts wanted to know what was in the offing. Why has this issue been pulled? What is it you're not telling us?

The irony was that throughout the industry, people had come to a number of different conclusions, all for the wrong reasons: Yes, something was up but no one suspected or speculated that it was a merger or a special loss provision. We indicated and they guessed that it was just a technical glitch. One potentially good thing was up, one bad thing, but neither one was decided, while the sands of our future continued to slip through an opening in the hourglass.

I phoned Carl, attempting to sound confident and cool. I filled him in on the pulled offering.

"That's not good."

"I know," I admitted. "It's terrible. But we can survive this." I continued. "We have simply got to bring our negotiations to a head. I know that you don't like to be rushed, but I've got a problem. I'm going to have to offer more detail on why I pulled the securities issue."

"How soon do we have to decide?" he asked.

I resisted the urge to tell him in the next thirty seconds. "Like, in the next three or four days. By Monday I would hope. I must know if I can announce a merger deal and identify the loss reserve as the reason for the pulled offering. If I can do that, it's going to play much better for our stock. Our stock price and yours are the basis for the fixed exchange rate. If our stock plummets with the reserve announcement, it will later make the deal look like a distressed sellout. I don't want that to happen, and it could jeopardize our merger."

"Right. A lot is riding on this."

A hell of a lot was riding on this. "You should also know that now that I must announce that I'm setting aside the special loan-loss reserves. I've also decided to write down some repossessed real estate we hold on our balance sheet and set aside other money to accelerate the shutdown of the Merchant Bank, a step that was intended to be part of our merger anyway." The Merchant Bank was the organizational identity attached to the numerous international securities and a few banking related activities that were struggling to perform up to expectations

I'd withheld any internal announcement about the disposition of the Merchant Bank pending a decision about the merger because I intended to announce it in tandem with my announcement of the merger. The combined announcement would suggest, by implication, that it was the natural and expected consequence of our monumental undertaking with Wells

Fargo. Without that triumph, I would just be issuing a list of incomprehensible goofs and disasters.

"We ought to be able to decide one way or another on our deal. If you feel we must wait, we'll have to wait. But I would really prefer that we go forward with the announcement of this transaction. We have everything decided and agreed. We have drafts of a definitive agreement. We have done so much and come so close. Why not go to our respective boards this weekend to finalize and sign the agreement so that it's done by Monday?"

I suspected that perhaps this response and my apparent impatience and anxiety for a decision would cause him to suspect that these matters were only the beginning of bigger issues with Security Pacific.

> *PATIENT – Business leaders can lose the support of their staff and all related parties and groups by reacting with impatience or lack of full consideration of the issues. In troubling situations, it is important to carefully reason and thoroughly think through decisions. A patient response should lead to better results and to maintaining the continuing support of all parties involved.*

He said he would think it through and call me back.

This was a terrible situation, and I knew I was trying to mask the bad with the good aspects of our company. I also was anxious to benefit from their strong capital position. While this approach could work out well, I had become undisciplined and somewhat deceptive in trying to make a bad situation look good. I was failing to fully consider the implications of the Wells deal not happening and I didn't think about how we would deal with the full exposure of our troubles. I was becoming undisciplined, flailing, and now begging instead of standing with strength and discipline no matter what happened to the Wells merger.

DISCIPLINED – It is important for business leaders to remain disciplined in their process and actions, even during the most uncertain or difficult times and situations.

In the meantime, I had a lot of thinking to do, and some heavy decisions to make. We would close in on an accurate loan loss reserve number; it was going to be significant, and I had to decide on the precise figure soon. Late on Thursday afternoon I decided that the following morning I would inform my key staff of my decision to shut down the Merchant Bank and inform its leader that as a result, he would be leaving the company.

I woke up on Friday, December 7, a day that will always live in infamy in my mind. I arrived at seven, made some notes, and called my staff into my office, most of whom had been largely excluded from news of my negotiations with Wells Fargo. I let them know what was up, and that I was confident that the Wells merger would take place as planned.

"As you might have guessed, whether we merge with Wells or not, I'm going to shut down the Merchant Bank." I confessed that I'd arrived at the decision some time ago but had held off on executing such a disruptive event pending a possible merger. I reiterated my reasons. The Merchant Bank, as ambitious and brilliant as the strategy was, was simply too unpredictable, difficult to manage and control, and too unprofitable. "It's hurting shareholder value. You know my heart was in this thing, and this was not a decision I made with any kind of joy."

I was restless. I found it hard to sit still, but I wasn't the type to pace. We were down to the wire. I longed for my phone to ring and to hear Carl on the other end of the line telling me effusively that he had decided to go forward with the merger.

PATIENT - During difficult or stressful times it is important for business leaders to remain patient, avoiding irrational thinking or vaguely considered decisions. Jumping to conclusions without carefully examining the facts, expectations, and risks can result in situations that are more difficult, costly, or risky to resolve.

Then at 11:30 a.m. my secretary put through a call. Great, I thought, the call I've been waiting for. I was positive he was going to say, "Let's go ahead. Let's get our boards together this weekend, sign the definitive agreement, and announce it on Monday." I picked up the phone. "Hi, how's it going?"

The response voice kicked in with uncharacteristic abruptness. "Say, you know Bob, this merger is a tremendous idea, just tremendous."

"Damned right it is."

Then the hammer came down. "But, unfortunately, after looking at it with a very positive spirit, we simply feel there are too many uncertainties."

Oh my God, I thought, it's not happening. Unbelievable. "Maybe I can clarify some points. What uncertainties, Carl?"

"Well, too many uncertainties about your company. Wells is a simple and straightforward organization. We're just meat and potatoes, very basic in what we do. Security Pacific, I've discovered, is a rather complex organization. It's hard to get a grasp on it. You know what I mean?"

My throat tightened. "What are you saying? You don't want to do the deal?"

"That's about the size of it. We just can't do the deal."

My guts churned. "This is undeniably a sour outcome to a lot of understanding between you and me and immense contemplated value for both of our investor shareholders. Our stocks will go off the charts. This is an enormous disappointment. Now I will have to go out and make my announcement without our planned merger. That's too bad and not what I was hoping for." Nothing but crummy news that will depress our stock and cause internal and external chaos, I thought.

"I understand, Bob. Like you, I was enthusiastic about this possibility. It just isn't going to happen."

This is not happening, I thought, as I imagined having to announce the huge loan loss reserve, the pulled offering, and turmoil in the Merchant Bank with no upside whatsoever. The sequence of events and timing was horrendous. I knew that I must now mask any personal expressions of disappointment and instead convey understanding and confidence in the future.

"Remain patient and calm," I thought. "Stay disciplined."

DISCIPLINED – A business leader's ability to undertake strong and effective decisions and actions requires the discipline to act and respond consistent with the company's established process and strategic thinking.

"Can you be specific about the uncertainties, Carl?" I asked humbly as a final plea. "Are you sure these uncertainties are so great that they should derail this merger?" I had crumbled in my reaction.

TRYING TO REMAIN POSITIVE

That weekend, we convened an emergency session of the Board of Directors. I don't know what was going through the minds of the Board members; perhaps they were certain they'd been called in to hear tremendous news of how the Wells merger would bring about enhancement to shareholder value. Feeling like one of Ingmar Bergman's scythe-wielding incarnations of Death itself, I opened with a frank apology for the shortness of the notice for this meeting. Then I promptly subjected them to a blizzard of disastrous points.

I was intent on being open and honest, to admit my accountability for our current situation, and then present them with a plan for the immediate future as well as the upcoming year. I wanted this important presentation to be focused on facts and to sound positive even though I was aware that our condition was the result of many negative ingredients. I pointed out that these factors, in part, included my failed management and leadership of the same team who were now expected to lead us into the future.

ETHICAL - *A defining character element of strong leadership is to display a high level of ethics, honesty, and truthfulness. Failing to convey the truth, misleading or distorting the facts to serve another business purpose or acting with dishonesty will ultimately lead to distrust and loss of leadership.*

ACCOUNTABLE – *It is important for business leaders to openly express their accountability for both positive and negative situations and results.*

I began by announcing that all expectations of a merger with Wells had fallen through for several reasons, not the least of which was our complexity and their inability to fully understand many of our activities, the uncertainty surrounding our credit difficulties, and the untraditional nature of many parts of the Merchant Bank. I noted that I had been very open with Wells, sharing with them the events and concerns we were experiencing. I noted that the openness of our discussions had, in some respects, been too much, too fast, and perhaps had shot us in the foot.

I noted as background for the future that we were experiencing an economic downturn that was impacting all of our key real estate markets. This, along with the impact of the FIRREA sourced changed regulatory definitions affecting our real estate collateral valuations, meant that we could expect continuing higher classified loan levels and higher loan losses.

The Board was then made aware of the facts that on Monday morning before the stock market opens we would announce that we were setting aside a $600 million addition to our loan loss reserve plus $200 million in reserve to shut down and dismantle the Merchant Bank; in addition, there would also be $100 million to write down a portion of the real estate we had taken back from defaulted borrowers.

Following many questions and concerns expressed by the Board members I offered them more detail behind the decision to close the Merchant Bank activities, an alternative they had been aware of for some time. I reminded them that this group was initially intended to expand our securities business worldwide in anticipation of United States legislative changes that would permit U.S. banks to be active in the underwriting and distributing of securities. We were giving up the expected future results in order to eliminate poor performance activities and to preserve capital, especially considering the current and anticipated increasing credit problems.

I outlined strategies for the immediate future. As part of the breakdown of the Merchant Bank, we would sell several subsidiaries; others would be managed down, closed, restructured, or reassigned to other units.

In addition, I added that we would also hopefully be able to preserve the company's dividend, which would certainly be under close regulatory scrutiny. I also noted that for the time being, we would cease acquisitions and not add any new credit commitments. "We have a very tough year ahead, but I believe we are up to the challenge."

I told them that because of all these matters, the regulatory agencies could be expected to step up their oversight of our bank. In this regard, I noted that the lead examiner from the Controller's Office had recently informed us that they had real concerns about our generally lower capital level, our larger than normal use of commercial paper for short-term funding, and the deficient loan-loss reserve levels. I added that we would concentrate on improving our standing with the regulatory community in the months ahead.

I further told the Board that we would experience a very poor fourth quarter and a collective year that was far from our expectations but that we were taking the steps we felt were necessary to provide a sounder base for the upcoming year.

There was nothing left to say, and after a brief discussion they accepted my explanation and approved the proposed special charge and the action plan for the upcoming year.

I desperately hoped that this five-day assault on Security Pacific — a pulled bond issue, scrapping my dream of a successful Merchant Bank, the heartbreaking phone call from Wells, an unprecedented and depressing emergency session of the Board of Directors, and the humiliation resulting from these charges that set the base for our worst year in recent memory — would represent an anomaly, a singular abyss from which we would emerge scathed but alive.

These events were unplanned, but I realized that it was necessary to remain fearless to unexpected responses and to realize that what is often seen as the expected is not always the reality of the occasion.

FEARLESS – A business leader's willingness to maintain confident, calm, and focused decisions and actions without evidence of fear is important in response to difficult situations.

COMMUNICATIVE – Business leaders should be skilled and willing to honestly and effectively communicate with individuals, small groups, and open public gatherings as well as to make large group presentations. Fear should be overcome through technique development, training, preparation, and practice.

As the weeks proceeded following this series of events, additional unexpected responses were experienced. We would, for the next three months, address a crisis in funding and liquidity that would put our bank on the edge of failure. The necessity for personally remaining calm, fearless, and focused would once again be seriously challenged.

4

HITTING BOTTOM

A TIME FOR REFLECTION

I t was about a week later in December 1990 that I sat silently at my desk, head in my hands, trying to understand the impact and reasons for the present situation. Why had we not learned the important lessons inherent in the disastrous savings and loan experience? This included the experience to be gained from watching the work of the characters of that period, including my time with Charles Keating, Abe Spiegel, and many others. I was deeply concerned that our bank might now be headed in the same direction as so many S&L charlatans, becoming another tragedy of the period.

In light of all the past experiences, I questioned why we had remained so committed to implementing highly leveraged growth strategies and aggressive real estate loan policies while holding only minimal levels of capital. I was aware that in carrying out these policies we had significantly benefited from maximum leverage in a historically strong economy. I also realized that this had been a successful method to maximize earnings and realize strong growth in our stock price. But even more relevant to our current situation, I had now become aware of how reckless and dangerous this was and how mistaken we were. We had placed too much of our money and confidence in real estate without considering that laws and economic markets can change.

> COMMITTED - *It is important for business leaders to hold a deep commitment and passion for the mission and strategic direction of the company. It is also important, however, to periodically refocus the commitment and moderate the passion to avoid difficulties resulting from decisions driven by passion or greed rather than reasoned thinking.*

Realizing the negative impact this flawed strategic thinking was having on the ongoing viability of our company, I looked back at my recent experiences when I sought a merger solution that could preserve our bank from its growing loan problems and weakened capital position. Rather than raising additional capital or restructuring the company immediately, both of which would have been costly, I sought a banking partner who had excess capital and with whom our combined merged cost savings could add significantly to our stock value. After several weeks of planning and discussions with Wells Fargo, this solution had suddenly collapsed. I was now left without any specific resolution.

I also knew that the recent December reserve announcement would bring to light everything we had attempted to do. My actions of the first year as CEO opened questioning by many, including the Board, as to my capability as the leader. Our future and expectations for the months ahead would be immediately challenged and placed in doubt.

I could see that everything we had done or wanted to do as part of my tenure would be challenged not only by those within the company but also by a plethora of affiliate groups, each of which had a specific interest in our bank. The microscopes of the press and stock analysts and all other questioning groups would be carefully directed at our management, my leadership, our past actions and strategies, and now poor results. All of this would become part of the company's as well as my personal legacy.

PATIENT – Business leaders should remain calm, steady, and patient when challenged by negative or threatening events.

DISCIPLINED – It is important that business leaders remain disciplined in managing and planning the process, response, and actions intended to correct or resolve difficult situations.

Notwithstanding these troubling circumstances, I acknowledged that it was critical for me to personally convey an atmosphere of positive confidence.. I had already seen several of my top managers express fear in their words and actions with respect to what this troubling situation might mean for the future of the bank and perhaps for them personally. I reminded them that it was critical to work through this difficult period and that we all must maintain and express confidence every day. Negativism or spreading a spirit of doom and gloom can be contagious to the entire organization, harming performance and restricting the expectations for the future.

CONFIDENT – Business leaders should be the primary messenger, conveying confidence with respect to a specific situation or the company's future. Leadership should not openly show or express a lack of confidence or concern for negative events or situations but instead focus on the intended resolution and the anticipated positive outcome.

COMMUNICATIVE – Business leaders should express and convey troubled situations in a constructive positive framework. This is a significant element in gaining and maintaining the confidence and support of all persons and groups of interest.

I was especially concerned about the impact our difficulties would have on our employee base around the world, our thousands of retirees, and our many investor shareholders. How would our millions of customers respond, I wondered? I had deep concerns regarding the impact on many affiliate groups that had a focused and important influence on our company. Would the rating agencies maintain our strong bond ratings or would the securities analysts lower our earnings expectations and recommend not holding our shares or debt instruments?

How might this impact the local and national community groups, state and local politicians, external accountants, numerous law groups, investment bankers, industry organizations, a variety of consultants, project and loan partners, plus hundreds of third-party contractors and suppliers? These groups were all relevant to the eventual success of our company as their actions and influence were often critical to the fulfillment of the business mission and related strategic action. They would all share concern about the impact our recent issues would have on our future.

> *COMMUNICATIVE - A good portion of a business leader's available time should be focused on effectively communicating and maintaining contact with the many persons and groups involved and related to the company. This practice should include listening to the views and thoughts of the participants and preparing them for uncertainties and changes in policy and events.*

I also recognized that in providing explanations about what had gone wrong, I should not offer any excuses. I could point to the economy, the overly aggressive regulators, newness on the job, the last CEO, a few bad employees, or whatever. I could even blame Keating and the S&Ls, but to do so would sound weak and shallow. It seemed necessary to assume personal accountability for the conditions and actions leading up to the charges. In reality, I saw a combination of many factors as bringing about the current situation, but I also was aware that most of them involved me. I would accept accountability for our weakened condition and would likewise accept the full responsibility to fix the problems.

ACCOUNTABLE – Business leaders should always be willing and capable of accepting full accountability for the failure to achieve intended results or for creating an environment that threatens the organization. Passing on accountability for failures to circumstantial situation or to other specific leaders within or outside the company is a poor leadership practice.

As a new CEO, I had been quickly thrust into the center of action whose web of necessary personal qualities extended well beyond my training. In late 1989, my predecessor had become gravely ill and incapable of continuing to direct the company after serving as its leader for over 10 years. This unexpected situation resulted in my sudden appointment as the bank's top officer in January 1990.

I was familiar with running operations and managing people in a limited environment where I had reasonable control of the staff and specifics of most situations, but this was different. I felt capable of leading the company, yet the current troubled circumstances as they had developed seemed well beyond my experience and pay grade. While I felt naively unprepared to deal with the difficulties, I knew that the responsibility for managing the solutions to this complex set of problems could not be delegated to others. When I looked around, there was no other person but me to lead the company through this troubled period.

I had very little formal university-based financial education or training. During my university experience I had only one course in accounting and no training in economics. My background in understanding financial issues and the economy had been formed through the experience of spending twenty-five years dealing with numerous bank and customer financial issues. Accounting, tax, financial, and capital market matters and challenges would be continually in front of me as we tried to move out of this trouble. I hoped that my experience- based learning would be sufficient to achieve positive results.

FINANCIAL UNDERSTANDING - It is essential that business leaders understand the application and implication of accounting, tax, financial and capital issues related to the company. The necessity of gaining a high level of understanding should not be avoided or delegated to subordinates.

I realized that each touch of this situation was important to our future and that every element had to be carefully managed if we were to emerge with as little damage as possible. We had to become passionate and committed to a well thought out structured solution for each matter or concern that could influence our company. Moving beyond the more recent situation, I needed to develop a clearly delineated strategic program to manage our next steps. But I didn't yet realize that there were more problems in our immediate future.

COMMITTED – Holding a commitment and passion for the company and the use of strategic thinking are important aspects of effective leadership.

OUR CREDIT RATING GETS DUMPED

During the first two weeks following the announcement of special charges, the press focused on criticism of our strategic thinking and leadership and demonstrated a lack of understanding of our company's larger issues. The federal regulators showed up to once again look over the quality of our loans and to better understand our decisions regarding loan charge-offs and reserving. They also wanted to better understand the impact that closing the Merchant Bank would have on business. On Wednesday of the first week, the Mayor called and wanted to understand the impact our actions might have with respect to closing branches, expected job losses, and maintaining community support.

The following Friday of the second week, we learned that our long-term debt rating was downgraded, negatively impacting the value of our outstanding bonds held by many creditors and investors. By the end of that week our stock price had declined nearly 20% to a two-year low. The stock analysts were in a near panic, and by the end of the month we suffered from several critical reports with two groups downgrading the bank to a sell recommendation of our stock. Their report was based upon the uncertain future earnings in an extremely weakening economy. It seemed that almost everything that could go wrong was approaching that objective.

It became obvious that managing the internal environment, including staff and employees, was a lot easier than gaining control of the outside world. I realized that I would have to redirect much of my attention to establishing better and clearer communications with the affiliate group, especially those outside of the institution, specifically the press but also the stock and credit rating analysts.

A week later, nearing the end of December, we were jarred into a state of real fear and near panic when Moody's and then Standard and Poor's, the principal bond rating agencies, announced a downgrade of our short-term debt rating from prime to non-prime. This rating is a respected quality determinant used by short-term investors with specific value in establishing the holdings of commercial paper. I had never met this group or any of its analysts, but for years we had maintained their prime rating, placing us among the least risky banks.

For several years through our holding company we had been issuing commercial paper with maturities of up to sixty days in order to fund its several subsidiary commercial loan activities. The bottom line impact of the rating downgrade was that mutual funds, the principal buyers of our commercial paper, were prohibited from holding more than 5% of non-prime grade commercial paper in their managed portfolios. Because of the downgrade, 95% of our $4 billion outstanding commercial paper would have to be redeemed and issued to new non–prime commercial paper buyers during the next sixty days. Quite an undertaking when you consider the uncertainty surrounding the financial weaknesses inherent in our recent announcements. This event magnified my concern for our future and suggested the need to exhibit positive confidence in our future more aggressively without conveying fear. Fear can be contagious, and I had already seen this expressed on the faces of a few of my key staff while discussing our alternatives. Even though my stomach turned with very deep concerns and uncertainty, I knew I would have to convey a "business as usual" attitude on a consistent basis.

Unfortunately, I had little knowledge of the significance of having a prime rating attached to our commercial paper or that this top rating status might be at risk as a result of announcing the special charges. If I had, early on, gained a better understanding of the workings of the rating agencies and the industry's holding limitations, I might have dedicated more time and effort to the consideration of our possible actions and alternatives. Perhaps we should have seen our sizable issuance of commercial paper as too risky to consider from the beginning. We did not anticipate or prepare for this event properly. I was surprised that our financial staff was equally unaware and did not properly consider or prepare for these risks. I was obviously very unhappy with their preparation and lack of planning.

I was, however, aware of the potential risk of maintaining high levels of short-term funding, and taking steps to reduce the level of this funding earlier in the year. I had initiated a plan promoting branch deposit growth and purchasing deposits of defunct S&Ls such as Gibraltar S&L. These steps had been particularly helpful in reducing the level of the bank's fed-funds issuance by nearly five-billion dollars but had no impact on the level of commercial paper issued by the holding company. Fed-funds are loans that are the exchange of excess funds between credit-worthy depository institutions.

FINANCIAL UNDERSTANDING– Business leaders should have sufficient financial knowledge to understand the potential financial impact of negative events, especially those matters that can impact the company's liquidity.

I was sure the rating agencies had been influenced by the poor press reports and the writings of Wall Street stock analysts. They all recognized the potential difficulties resulting from the declining economy, the implementation of FIRREA, and failing real estate values. It was also clear that as the result of short-term funding exposure, we had become the subject of conversation and street talk, none of which was positive.

We had a sixty-day period to find new commercial paper buyers and avoid losing our liquidity, which would effectively make it impossible to settle transactions with other banks and securities firms. We would be out of cash and unable to survive without help. Such an event could force us to go the Federal Reserve Discount Window to obtain sufficient emergency cash to survive. This would have to be a last-ditch desperation move.

It was generally believed by many of my staff that it would be extremely difficult to find enough new commercial paper investors in such a short period to replace the previous holders. Beyond the questionable demand for our non–prime commercial paper, it was also clear that, while not particularly relevant under the present circumstances, our funding costs would be significantly increased.

Compounding the entire situation was the instability of our commercial paper issuing staff. They had no loyalty, smelled our troubles, and wanted to be paid a substantial bonus to complete the commercial paper refunding challenge. At the time, their boss was on a hunting vacation in Mexico and was out of contact. In this environment, I was becoming very annoyed. While I knew I could go to any one of several outside commercial paper brokers if necessary, that would not be a good decision because of the short time window available to complete the refunding. Notwithstanding the potential impact of the funding risk, I drew a hard but high-risk line and told our fifteen or so staff brokers to quit if they didn't like their current financial arrangement.

COMMITTED – Business leaders should build an environment in which the company and its well-being are leading objectives and strong priorities for managers and employees at all levels. It is essential that this priority outweighs any consideration of potential personal gain.

They all showed up for work that week and it seemed that my threat worked, even though the whole event increased my anxiety about survival. I thought of them as a staff whom I would keep only until this crisis was over. When we were out of the woods, I would make sure they would all be fired and replaced with new personnel. Obviously, the relationship between these brokers and the bank was terrible, and it wasn't enhanced by my attitude or actions.

The commercial paper refunding process went well over the first three weeks as we completed refunding over a billion dollars of our $4 billion exposure. I knew that offering a higher interest rate for what had become non–prime higher risk commercial paper would attract some of the low-hanging investor fruit initially. However, I was convinced that it would then become more difficult to place in the coming weeks because the market for this non–prime commercial paper was very thin, with only a limited number of potential investors. I was unsure that there was enough market for the entire $4 billion we needed to reissue.

At the end of the first 30 days we were keeping up with the commercial paper refunding, but the maturities of the commercial paper were weighted to the end of the period. I now realized we would need a miracle to refinance all the paper within that time frame, since demand for the offerings was diminishing, notwithstanding the increased pricing. I realized that I would more than likely need some outside help to keep the bank funded.

To fill the expected void, we considered using available emergency back-up banking credit lines, but we understood that these lines were historically only rarely employed to cover short-term cash needs of a few days. If we used this source of funding, we had no means to pay the borrowings back in a short-time frame. Additionally, continued use of these credit lines would send out alarms to other banks and securities firms about our troubles. We needed a longer-term solution to obtain the necessary new funding.

We also considered selling large blocks of loans but knew that, once again, a wholesale liquidation of our loan portfolio would send out crisis alarms. I was becoming disappointed that the financial staff had not prepared for such situations, nor were they effectively coming up with workable solutions. However, one action was helpful. We called a halt to initiating new credits or credit lines and limited the use of the outstanding lines when possible. This would have a positive impact on our available cash.

ORGANIZED - The ability for business leaders to organize the personnel and resources necessary to fulfill both short- and long-term strategies and solve problems is an important leadership quality.

SELECTIVE – The ability of business leaders to effectively select and organize an intelligent experienced staff is a significant consideration in developing the team necessary to achieve the best results.

About a month into the refunding, we were made aware and were stunned by another equally significant negative event. We were advised by Goldman Saks, our security under-writers, that we would have to immediately redeem a $500 million floating auction rate preferred stock that was issued as part of our capital structure. I couldn't believe that our financial staff hadn't become aware of or anticipated this event and developed a plan to deal with the situation.

This unique capital item was, according to its terms, refunded every week by its holders based upon an auction for the interest rate covering the next week. Because of only limited buyers and the rating downgrade, we were informed that there were no buyers, at any price, for our upcoming weekly auction. The instruments could not be reissued or sold and therefore the outstanding $500 million of preferred stock would have to be redeemed by the beginning of the next week. I assumed that without bidders the issue was being temporarily held by Goldman Saks, and they wanted out. The hole we were in had just gotten a lot darker and deeper. Fortunately, this redemption occurred at a high point in the cash cycle, and we were able to meet the repayment demand. Our need for cash, however, just got bigger. My passion to remedy this situation intensified.

COMMITTED – It is significant for business leaders to remain committed and passionate in fulfilling the company's mission, notwithstanding troubling situations.

We had fortunately maintained a long-term relationship with the investment banking firm Credit Suisse First Boston (CSFB). They knew our company and our people and were very cognizant of our growing funding problems. They also knew that our structure of non–banking subsidiary finance companies had historically had strong earnings, top management, and significant value. In many respects, they were our strongest ally and were interested in our continued viability. I realized that business friends do matter when times get tough.

With days advancing quickly, I called an emergency meeting of my staff to consider the options if we failed to replace the entire $4 billion of maturing commercial paper as well as the new $500 million auction rate preferred. Reviewing our cash flow and the potential short-term markets, we estimated that our refunding effort could fall as much as a billion dollars short over the remaining thirty days of commercial paper reissuance.

As a result, we knew it was essential to identify and consider alternate forms of financing for that amount. Because of the uncertainty associated with this entire effort, we agreed that we should add an additional $250 million to ensure we would successfully refund our operation and retain liquidity.

After considerable discussion, CSFB said they would be willing to provide a six-month $1.25 billion credit line if we were willing to secure this credit with the stock of all of our seven non-bank finance companies operated as part of our holding company. It was these same finance company subsidiaries that had been funded by the issuance of the commercial paper. With time running out to meet our objectives, I gave a quick thumbs-up to their refunding plan. Under the circumstances their fees would be substantial, but their stated pricing gave value to our long-term relationship and I felt made the deal fair to both parties.

The funding strategy of borrowing short-term and lending long-term through the finance companies had for many years provided us with an advantage in terms of a better interest rate spread and greater earnings. We had been funding longer term finance company loans with short- term commercial paper issued through the parent holding company. A substantial spread advantage was gained through this arbitrage, but this was a high-risk decision that was collapsing at our feet.

Before the greater portion of refunding was due, we had agreed to all the terms of the CSFB financing and closed the transaction. On the sixtieth day since the credit rating downgrade, we had fully completed the commercial paper and preferred stock redemptions with a cash margin of only $50 million. We had retained liquidity and avoided a funding failure, yet we had only done so with the support and long relationship developed over the years with CSFB. We now had sufficient time to work out long-term solutions to our funding issues.

DECISIVE - Business leaders should act decisively in making business decisions. When responding with decisive action there should be consideration of the history of prior practices, current facts, and potential risks of the decision.

FAIR – Business leaders should maintain long-term fair and equitable relationships with the many affiliate groups. The strength of these relationships and the circumstances often outweigh many other factors when considering fairness and equity.

ETHICAL – Business leader should establish, act, and communicate with staff and affiliate groups applying ethical values, honesty, and truthfulness both personally and in the business actions and decisions.

While the press was generally unaware of the difficulty we had faced in refunding, they seemed to be more concerned about our long-term expectations. We were aware but had not yet openly discussed the fact that a large concentration of our loans had been made to real estate developers for real estate land and development purposes. I didn't think that the press was fully aware of the difficulties we faced or had yet recognized that a weakened economy and FIRREA regulations were putting increasing stress in our loan portfolio.

It wasn't long, however, before many in the press began to challenge our ability to overcome the credit problems and began hinting that we could face even greater problems in the months ahead. Their thoughts were mirrored by an increased concern on the part of the banking regulators.

I knew that my time in the months ahead would have to be focused on improving their knowledge of our strengths and the efforts we were making to once again return to normalcy. I wanted them to see the positives along with the glitches in our company. At the same time the securities analysts, who regularly cast opinions on the future of our stock, were beginning to question the expectations for future earnings, including the growing level of troubled loans. The outside world now had us under a microscope that we knew would not go away quickly. Yet I remained confident about our future although somewhat cautious and reserved as to when it could realize its potential.

> *CONFIDENT - A fundamental ingredient of business leaders is to naturally convey to all parties and groups a high level of confidence in the company and its future. Conveying negative feelings or lost confidence can portray negativism. Positive confidence is generally reflected in the voice, tone, expressions, and body language of the leaders. Better leaders develop techniques to minimize any external expression other than full confidence in the situation or intended actions of the company.*

THE HAWAIIAN EXTRAVAGANZA

This period was an early low point in my experience as the new CEO and seemed to be a long distance from the exciting events I had experienced just two years prior. How, I wondered, had so much changed so fast for our industry and bank? It was becoming clear that our long period of success and growing complacency could have motivated our willingness to assume the unhealthy risks of our growing real estate loan portfolio. This complacency began with good times in which we felt we were at the top of our game.

During the 1980's the arrogance of bankers and of our bank in particular was leviathan in scope. The queasy extravagance of the time was epitomized by the American Bankers Association's annual conventions, which during that period could attract up to 15,000 senior bankers and people who wanted to do business with this banking group. These were elaborate brag-fests of leisure and self-congratulation — a high-class Mardi Gras for financiers. Queues of shiny black and white limousines stretched around resort hotels like glittering angels cascading up and down Jacob's ladder, prepared to shepherd banking and corporate executives from golf course to swimming pool to elaborate dinners and then back again.

Prestige figured powerfully in this equation. It was not only part of our strategy but promoted tremendous public relations to participate in this megalomaniacal show and talk with an array of congressional members, senators, lobbyists, deal-makers, government regulators, and luminaries. The bank-sponsored parties were often pretentious as competitors tried to outdo one another. Some banks set up private tours to visit local historical landmarks. Parties were hosted at the five-star hotels or clubs where top-bill entertainment was provided. Such lavish self-indulgence was beyond the pale.

These conventions were routinely held in New York, Chicago, New Orleans, Hawaii, and other major U.S. cities. Naturally, there was intense rivalry among the top banks to see which institution could host the most exorbitant party. Competition was stiff.

It was in 1988 that our top executives, all adorned in a common Hawaiian shirt and blue blazers, stood at the door shaking hands and welcoming people to a grand seaside suite at Hawaii's Colony Surf Hotel and later at a private mansion on Kahala Beach. Snow-capped confections, succulent pastries, ice molds of our logo, and a full bar were all displayed beneath a lighting configuration that would humble Pink Floyd.

Braggadocio masked idle chatter that would have made Donald Trump's palms sweat. Visions of grandeur danced in our heads as we enthusiastically discussed deals, fantasized the next technological advance, or compared itineraries of upcoming travel. These events were exhilarating with promise and blind to the inevitable eventuality of an economic downturn.

As we sat down at our dinner event with many of our corporate clients and prospects, a major corporate Chief Financial Officer at my table asked me what we were up to.

I shrugged and answered as if all we did was routine. "Now that the securities-oriented Merchant Bank is active we're doing major transactions virtually all over the world. Our derivative and swaps operations are top rated internationally, and we just made a multi-million-dollar loan to help finance a Major League baseball team. We're involved in most of the Leveraged Buy-Out deals as a bank lender, and we are one of the premier lenders in California real estate. We're also experimenting with video-banking. Soon you'll be able to sit down at your home computer to pay bills and do your banking or to have a face-to-face talk with a stockbroker, trade bonds, or conduct a swap transaction in any currency, twenty-four hours a day."

It was a shameless answer; I was blowing smoke up his ass. But in this rarefied atmosphere, the urge to boast was irresistible.

Following the party, I kibitzed with other executives beneath a grand ice sculpture. We bathed in the warm glow of what felt like a very successful evening. Nevertheless, our Chief Credit Officer was beating the gong of doom, as he often did. His voice was monochromatic and his body language heavy with unwelcome prophesy as he spoke of dark clouds on the horizon.

I, for one, was interested in hearing what he had to say.

He went on, "The market share of the top-rated banks' commercial loans has shrunk from 35% to roughly 20%, so while we slap ourselves on the back so enjoyably, believing we are important, it may ultimately turn out that we are not all that important because what happens is there is always a better mousetrap invented. Someone will find a better and cheaper way to provide any form of financing to people who need it. In this process, we're taking on higher risks and supporting ourselves with less and less capital."

I responded, "capital is always available; it's just a matter of what the price, terms, and conditions are, and how they affect the ultimate purpose and use of that capital. If you assume a little more risk, with a little more leverage, you'll just pay a little more for your capital."

He remained unconvinced and stoic. "We'll see. Because of our victories and good results, I sense a certain conceit; we've forgotten the rudimentary importance of a strong capital base. We are highly leveraged but believe we are too big to fail and will always be able to attract capital. One of the weaknesses in this strategy is that we've become less concerned about the basics — capital and funding."

Perhaps he had a rare premonition to the events of late 1990.

PROTECTIVE - It is important for business leaders to maintain quality in the assets, service, and operations of the company. Most importantly, this protective nature includes sound practices, valuation, and maintaining adequate supporting capital.

"We don't have to be concerned with that right now," I commented. "That's the beauty of this phase. We can always get capital and we can always get funded."

As I was soon to realize, it would have been much better if in addition to talking I had been willing to learn as I listened.

He frowned. "It's rather natural and a tendency that when things are going well and everyone is comfortable for an individual, an institution, or even an entire industry to become somewhat self-pleased."

Although we didn't want to believe it, he was correct; in fact, he was dead on. The wimps of the 80s, those who were aware and cautious of risks, were about to become the heroes of the 90s: the market leaders, the top of the heap. Their prudence and restraint during this period of excess positioned them for success in what would be the greatest consolidation and highest market valuation era in banking history. Those who sought high-risk ventures and aggressive growth would be the victims, sucked up into the belly of the wimps. We had clearly become undisciplined in assessing the underlying risks of our overly aggressive strategies.

DISCIPLINED – It is important for business leaders to be disciplined in maintaining the commitment to well thought out and conceived company strategies, decisions, and intended actions that can be effective in both good times and bad. All involved are more inclined to follow and respond to disciplined consistent business leaders.

It appears that we had become overwhelmed with our importance and success as well as not accepted the wisdom offered by our Chief Credit Officer. It was evident that in any gathering it was important not only to speak and discuss but also to listen and learn. There is a lot to be gained from those whose experience and qualities give them a greater knowledge of the full situation.

5

WHAT WENT WRONG?

THE TRUMP EXPERIENCE

At the genesis of our problems in the early 90's was our desire to strategically and aggressively undertake the role of being the leading lender to real estate developers. We had accumulated a long list of major real estate moguls, including those who participated in our annual Palm Desert based Vintage Country Club event as our customers. We also had participated with many of these leaders in transactions in which we were a lender-partner, collecting interest as well as sharing in the project's profits. We had built a loan portfolio with a concentration of loans for warehousing land and the build-out of residential tracts, condos, small commercial and industrial properties, and resorts.

We held over $17 billion in loans for holding land and the development of these properties, including about $4 billion of mini-perm loans or short maturity, fixed rate loans on commercial properties. This group of loans accounted for nearly a quarter of our total loan portfolio and amounted to about four times our total capital level. With this interest in real estate we were attractive to developers who wanted to benefit or get their piece of the West Coast real estate growth opportunities.

Donald Trump was already a known commodity to most real estate lenders and investors around the world. Everyone understood that he had a large ego and a desire for importance and financial success. For several years he had successfully developed skyscrapers in New York and other major world cities. In his most recent effort to grow his wealth and recognition, he had labored to revitalize the appeal of Atlantic City with grand style casino-hotels, and an expressed intent to halt the city's progressive decay.

When I first met with Trump he had already been heralded by many as a financial and real estate genius who seemed to be at the leading edge of everything.

Earlier that year he'd made an appointment to see me through some of my staff, who had been overwhelmed by his personality. They thought he was enigmatic, luminous, and personally charming.

I didn't know what he had in mind for Security Pacific, and when he stepped into my office, I greeted him with cautious expectations.

He carried a Super Star aura around him, the effervescent stamp of a studied deal-maker, and an ability to communicate and inspire the belief of others in his personal vision. He could no doubt have been an evangelist.

Unfortunately, by now it was well established among the investment community that charismatic though he was, Trump was building a house of cards. I was optimistic but I was intent on being extremely cautious.

"What's on your mind, Donald?" I opened our discussion following a warm handshake.

COMMUNICATIVE – Notwithstanding prior poor experience or objectionable individual traits of meeting contacts, business leaders should convey a spirited level of warmth and congeniality. Warm greetings and nonconfrontational discussion are preferred methods in conducting potentially unattractive personal meetings.

His dimples flashing, waving a finger at me, he said, "I want you, I want Security Pacific. I need Security Pacific."

"Why us?" I said, trying to screw up my face into a picture of wonder.

"Something big, really big." With the sincerity of the sages, he told me, "The reason I want Security Pacific is that I want a real, true, and honest to God West Coast bank to lead the charge."

I became quickly aware and recognized that with this introductory statement what he really wanted was more money.

"How much?"

"Fifty million will get this deal started."

Fifty million was the high end of our "house" limit or the maximum amount we would lend to any one borrower or any one deal. It was almost as if he could read our minds. And if we would lend it, he would build it, whatever it was. And he still had not told me what it was. "Donald," I said, wonder completely erased from me now, "What exactly do you have up your sleeve?"

"The idea is to revitalize the Ambassador Hotel area. You know, where Bobby Kennedy was assassinated."

We knew all right.

"Now," Trump continued, "I know that area is not in exactly tip-top shape, but all that's going to change as I put my expertise to it. When this baby is in, there's no telling how much of a draw it's going to be as a more desirable community."

"There's no telling," I echoed, as Trump unrolled a map.

It was now obvious that he was only touting an idea, a concept. He had no plans, no presentation, just an idea and a one-page personal financial statement.

"You see? Its right smack on the edge of the business district."

"Well, it used to be."

"And it will be again—when my project is complete."

"We will be putting up a 124-story building to house condos, a five-star hotel along with five-star restaurants, a massive retail space, and lots of commercial offices. It all goes together and becomes a city within a city. We'll get the plans, permits, and boom, we're off and running. This will become the new center of downtown Los Angeles."

I listened, stopping short of drawing any conclusions on this deal, but I expressed my reservations. I didn't tell him there was something faintly morbid about the entire enterprise. But I did discuss the demographic uncertainties. "Donald, my sense of it is that Security Pacific would not be overly anxious to participate in the financing of that particular development in that depressed area. This is a pioneering effort on your part."

"Depressed area now, sure," he said with some exasperation. "That's exactly why the deal makes sense. I can buy the land cheap. Isn't that the idea behind renovation? You take something that is maybe not so good and work it, build it, and make it great. There's something special about the Ambassador Hotel. I'm going to make it great again."

I didn't think it was such a good idea. "Not to pop your balloon, but that precinct is a miserable, terrible, decaying area. Every respectable retail establishment has shut down, the commercial businesses have moved out, and it's being settled predominantly by only the lowest-income immigrants from Central America and Asia. I have nothing against immigrants but, honest to God, I feel it's not a very good idea. We would most likely not put our money into a project of that kind."

"You know Mr. Trump, even if we were to consider participation, we would need your personal guarantee of a deal like this. We would need you to support and back up repayment if the deal never materialized."

"Oh, I understand. But I don't guarantee deals that are that small. Anyway, I have a lot of big-time assets to back this up. I gave you my financial statement."

"I know, but there are no details on this one page and very few liquid assets."

Trump, never disheartened but maybe even a little surprised continued, "but this is an easy deal for a bank of your stature and size."

After his attempt to dazzle us, my answer remained the same. I didn't like the deal, with or without any guarantee.

Following the meeting, my colleagues seemed shell-shocked when I told them.

"You said no to Donald Trump?"

"No, I didn't say 'no' to Donald Trump, but I didn't say yes either. I just don't like this deal. We would be the ones at risk if the project never materialized. I certainly hope the account officer gets that message and doesn't think anything else. I told Trump I did not think the loan was a good idea. I just don't think that is the sort of deal we want to do. I don't like the project, I don't like the location, and Trump is leveraged up to his ass with everybody."

"Yeah, but he's Donald Trump. And he's come to Security Pacific; he wants us."

"Well, we can't be too naïve. He's probably approached a dozen banks, including Wells Fargo and Bank of America, and told all of them that they're special. That's how developers swing these deals, they try to play us off against one another. They create curiosity, friction, and envy. The more he can finance, the more value there is in his equity in the deal. All he wants is the front money for plans and permits. He probably doesn't have a dime in this deal other than plane fare out West. He is only involved to promote the concept, financing, and community politics. He even said this deal was too small for his personal guarantee."

> PROTECTIVE – *Business leaders should consider the risks of the project and its developer as well as the impact of weakened economic circumstances. Relying on the possibility of escape or the easy mitigation of risk in aggressive transactions is an assumption that should be avoided.*

"But he's Donald Trump," the account officer whined again.

"So?" I said. "This fever to be a part of prestigious deal, to be able to say, 'I'm with Trump' is a salient factor in his strategy and has unhinged many a bank." This star-struck and persuasive performance is the downside of the entrepreneurial spirit we encourage at Security Pacific.

The account officer was heartbroken and implored me to reconsider. "Bob, deals like this, if they succeed, will catapult us up the ladder. Everybody will want to bring their deal to us."

"It's like playing the lotto," I told them. "This project is a $50 million spin of the Donald Trump Wheel of Fortune, with many spaces marked 'you lose.' And that's just for starters — that barely pays for the development plans."

"But when a guy like Trump gets into trouble, he can refinance to pay us back."

Oh, I thought, that's a fool's trap. "When a guy like Trump gets into trouble, he can no longer borrow because no institution will lend to him."

Trump had succeeded in part because of charisma. He was passionate and professionally presented convincing scenarios; he could compel and dazzle entire board rooms with the ardor of a True Believer. Trump would never dare diagram a serious billion-dollar deal on a Stick-It notepad like some of the other developers, but in this case, he really didn't give us much information. He seemed to stay totally conceptual and without the details that I didn't think he really had. After our meeting, there was only one convincing conclusion: he would easily accept a lot of our money that he might never be able to repay.

As a lender, no matter how glamorous the person is on the other side of the table, you look to the borrower to have both primary and alternate sources of repayment. And while Trump presented a financial statement with many million dollars net worth, the ability for him to bail out even this project was limited. He was fully leveraged, without liquidity, with a net worth built around assets of questionable value.

Four months later I was flabbergasted to see a credit report that indicated our account officers had lent $10 million to something called Taj Mahal Enterprises.

"What's this for?" I asked my Chief Credit Officer.

"Oh, that's Donald Trump's empire."

"No, no, no," I said. "Didn't anyone listen?"

I raised holy hell. "What was going through those guys' heads? Why didn't someone tell me about this before we committed?"

"It's for part of an initial study on the feasibility of restoring the Ambassador Hotel."

"I don't need $10 million to explain the feasibility of that: it's zero."

COMMUNICATIVE – Business leaders should fully and clearly express opinions and intentions to all involved in order to avoid any misunderstandings or unintended actions. Communications on matters that do not convey the proper message are generally the fault of the communicator. Individual leaders should develop techniques to express the proper message in clear and understandable terms.

Two years later we wrote the whole thing off. It was a loss. After a number of legal battles and liquidation sales, the L.A. School District took over the property and in 2009 built a learning center in what still remains a drug-infested depressed area.

BIG TIME REAL ESTATE DEVELOPERS

As our business with the real estate developers grew, some sought opportunities in other states and occasionally other countries. One of those developers. Chris Hemmeter, was a Southern California resident who had become a close friend of our then CEO. He was purported to have conceived the so-called "Destination Resort," where the whole family, including kids, could be attracted to spend their entire vacation. It was a place full of continual entertainment and activities. Only the family pets would have to be left behind; grandmas and nannies were welcome.

Hemmeter was the Orange County real estate developer to whom it was difficult to say no. Chris was the preeminent hotel and resort developer in Hawaii at the time and had an uncanny ability to talk banks into wanting to be part of his destination resort concept. "You take your family, and everything you ever dreamed or fantasized is right smack on the premises; golf courses, waterfalls, swimming pools, gift shops, dolphin pools, fountains of gold and Perrier-filled saunas."

Tall and suave, he had enthusiasm that was contagious, and his dreams were enormously appealing. Unfortunately, he had to use a lot of the bankers' money to make them come true. And, as with Trump, there was no escape hatch for creditors if the dream collapsed.

Around this time, he was pushing us hard for a loan to finance the construction of a Westin-operated destination resort on Kauai. His presentation was laid back, self-assured, and engaging.

His preferred method of persuasion was to hijack our imaginations: "Irresistible is the word. Cascading waterfalls in an open-air courtyard featuring one of the biggest trees you've ever seen, sitting majestically on a small island in the middle of a pond full of ducks and koi fish, and this is only where you register. That's the lobby! We haven't even talked about the Action Core."

He was an imaginative genius who'd put considerable time and money into devising plans, schematics, renderings, and proposals that were scintillating to the eye. Unlike Trump, he totally engaged us in both the concept and the detail.

"Natural saunas, cobblestone walkways lined with eucalyptus trees, and luminaries." Chris knew our leaders, and we all loved golf. He was careful to emphasize the two signature golf courses to be financed as part of the project. "These aren't your ordinary resort-type golf courses; they are Professional Golf Association quality and very challenging. We are going to construct a network of man-made waterways or canals that weave throughout the complex. Boats will ferry entire families along these canals, taking them either to one of the most unique restaurants in all of Hawaii or a small, very special zoo featuring exotics."

Oh boy, I thought, he is going to make it very difficult to say no.

"Every weekday at dusk, our staff will redefine the Hawaiian luau. This Kauai resort will be a feast for the senses, a tropical oasis situated between those two eighteen-hole golf courses," he repeated. "Our swimming pools will have themes. And some of our pools are special because they are not for people. No, not these pools; they will be home to an array of the most exotic fish you've ever seen. Sip a mai tai and watch the pretty fish. The beauty will be humbling."

The numbers were humbling. Chris wanted a $100 million loan. Given his performance history and the charm of the deal, I felt confident we could probably sell the loan down to our $50 million house limit.

"The resort will have an Asian theme. We are going to purchase and showcase art from the Orient. Vases, tapestries, Buddhas — that type of thing."

I wondered if this concept would make it easier to sell the resort to the Japanese if things didn't work out. The Japanese were now buying many hotels in Hawaii. There was an inflated market. Entrepreneurs were rapidly creating these fantastic properties and then selling them at enormous profits.

"Anything the customer wants will be provided," he continued, "including a full array of swimwear, sports equipment, even sunburn remedies. Purchase or rent it on the spot and sign it to the room."

Sign it to Security Pacific, I thought.

While his personality was commanding, the amount of dollars the banks were lending relative to the fundamentals of credit to fund his projects was excessive. We would be funding his dreams and hoping for the cash flow or eventual sale of the property to repay us.

He somberly admitted that the cost of the project and financing requirements were a lot to ask for. "I know it's a lot of money," He said frankly, "but look at the plan. It's all here; the only thing left to do is build the damn thing."

With some reluctance, I was taken in and sold on what was a breathtaking concept. Besides, I thought, if we were tumbling into another credit trap, we could always sell off the portion of this transaction we don't want to hold.

The other side of operating on a disciplined, controlled basis is to become undisciplined in relation to reasoned thinking in the process of a risk-versus-reward evaluation. I had become overconfident and drawn in by the adventure story of a fast-talking real estate developer who could spin straw into silk.

DISCIPLINED – It is important for business leaders to remain disciplined in applying historically accepted company standards and policies.

With some trepidation, we ultimately took part in the financing of the Hemmeter project. The rudiments of credit were increasingly compromised by our lenders as we ventured into these multi-hundred-million-dollar loans; they'd become very transaction-oriented. This fervor to be part of every prestigious transaction no matter how seductive the vision was as compelling as it was unhealthy for an institution like Security Pacific. We had been caught in the momentum of "bigger is always better" trap.

The other side of confidence is overconfidence, which can result in ill-conceived and poorly thought out decisions. With the strong bank results of the 1980's we were riding high with confidence in our real estate loan quality and the consistently strong results evident in the growth of

California. Our risk consciousness and our normally cautious nature were being pushed aside and lost.

> CONFIDENT – *Business leaders should not become overconfident during prolonged periods of strong business results or continuing economic growth.*

Why did this deal get made while Trump and others didn't get our blessing? The Trump idea was just that, an idea that had not been fully developed. He was seeking front money for the idea, not money to construct the project. In addition, the Ambassador development was a pioneering effort to change a downtrodden part of the city, while the Kauai development was to meet the established demand for hotel accommodations on the island. We were also aware that there were Japanese buyers standing in the wings to potentially take us out of the Hemmeter project.

Not only was Hemmeter fortunate in terms of his timing but he presentation overwhelmed us with charm, excitement, detail and seemed to fit-in with our commitment to growth. It also hit us on our growth swing before the Trump deal and before we were "grounded" by our troubles and worries that stanched our loan originations.

Fortunately, we got all our money back on this Kauai resort project, albeit at the last minute and with a little pain. When economic troubles grew, and occupancy stalled, they managed to sell the twin golf courses at the Westin Kauai and partially repay the loan which went to the portions we had subsequently sold to other lenders. But there remained a $50 million portion of the loan secured by the hotel, which we held. In time, as cash flow shortfalls remained, the hotel was sold separately to Japanese investors and the loan, after an extended period without any payment of interest, was eventually repaid. This good fortune was not so easily obtained a year later as the real estate market and resort activity continued to collapse in a deep economic downturn.

6

KEEPING FAITH WITH THE PUBLIC

CONFRONTING THE PRESS

When a public company experiences unanticipated negative financial results, undertakes out of the ordinary action or is involved in unanticipated changes, it is important and legally necessary to communicate these developments quickly to those impacted by the company. Among these sources, the press is particularly relevant because their work carries the information or message to a broad spectrum of others, including the general public.

Also, particularly important is the timeliness of communicating similar matters to the security analysts, who routinely analyze, evaluate, and report the pros and cons of stock ownership of individual companies. Additionally, it is necessary to communicate with the major rating agencies who evaluate the company on behalf of debt holders and bank creditors.

Soon after the end of each quarter, we would routinely conference with the press to give them an update on our results and other important operational challenges or changes. Under certain circumstances, we would also meet with individual members of the press and others, one on one, to discuss events and actions in more detail.

In early 1991 it seemed imperative, following our year end 1990 announcement of special changes, to meet formally with the press, analysts, and rating groups as soon as possible. This action was advisable to clarify any questions they might have and to offer a view of expectations for the period ahead. Even with some urgency to fully inform these groups, I decided that it would be in our collective best interest to wait until the commercial paper refunding effort was complete and the year end 1990 results were finalized. Under all the circumstances, I felt that this delay would permit the presentation of a more positive, stable outlook for our future.

We made arrangement for a New York combined institutional investor, analyst, rating agency and press meeting at the Waldorf Astoria Hotel in late- February 1991. I was expecting a tough environment in light of the special charges, a poor year, and our recent funding difficulties. I knew that expressing a positive future outlook would be extremely challenging. I was disappointed that I could not tell them of the future we had anticipated if we had been able to consummate a merger with Wells Fargo. Instead, I knew that they would all be left with concerns and doubts about the year ahead.

The meeting was scheduled to begin at 10:00 a.m. in the larger meeting hall of the hotel with expectations of perhaps 150 to 200 attendees. After a formal presentation describing the more recent experiences of the fourth quarter. including our special charges and an overall poor 1990, I intended to convey a positive outlook for the future expectations for Security Pacific. I believed the outlook for the year was positive, but I knew that it was dependent on a recovering economy, relaxed regulatory oversight, and the positive spirit of our employees along with the continuing loyalty of our customers. Following this presentation, we planned to open the floor to questions and later to offer a more intimate meeting at which we would address more specific questions on the record.

As part of the presentation, I knew it was necessary to present an honest, transparent portrayal of the circumstances that had evolved from the troubled economy, California real estate difficulties, and more details surrounding the prior year's special charges. I would not, however, discuss the missed opportunity of the aborted Wells Fargo merger. I assumed that someone in the attending group might, however, pose a question about merger possibilities in the future. Most all the attendees would be aware that any possible combination would be limited to Wells Fargo, Bank of America, and First Interstate Bank because of multi-state banking limitations prescribed in the McFadden Act.

My objective was to clarify any earnings and liquidity uncertainties and convey confidence that Security Pacific had both a positive earnings and growth potential. This would be a tough challenge considering the expectation of continuing economic difficulties and the prolonged impact such conditions might have on our already troubled real estate loan portfolio. Overall, I needed to calm any fears they might have about our current stability and to illustrate the value inherent in the franchise's future.

After formally reviewing the past year and the troubles we had overcome; I continued by showing several slides clarifying the substance of our core retail banking business and its earning power. This core business had grown to produce an annual $2 billion pretax, pre-reserve cash flow. This was a strong insurance policy for our entire operation and was an important slide.

The presentation offered an understanding of the financial impact and anticipated benefits of shuttering the Merchant Bank and the changed business emphasis as a result of restricting real estate loans. I knew that my arguments and the validity of the details were weak in some areas, but I was sure that the collective changes would soften any concern this group might have for more trouble in the new year.

I noted the expectations for the upcoming months. In addition to our core retail banking business, our more significant earnings would result from our non-bank finance company activities. These areas were expected to produce over a half-billion dollars in annual cash flow. I expressed the fact that our expectations were dependent on our economic forecast, which called for a gradual economic recovery over the balance of the year. I expressed the feeling that we anticipated that these positive operations would most likely ease the regulatory pressure in the months ahead. My expectations for both the economy and regulator precepts turned out to be wrong by a significant factor.

I was deeply concerned, however, about the results stemming from a recently conducted internal analysis and review of our bank's loan portfolio conducted during January and February. This study reviewed our real estate loans, under the FIRREA rules to establish our expectation of future losses. We examined the portfolio using both "most likely" and "worst-case" scenarios. Under the "worst-case" scenario, we had based our assumptions on our recent experience, which indicated a near 30% write-down of troubled real estate loans when FIRREA's revised appraisal standards were strictly applied.

A review of these results had increased my concern. If the economy didn't improve significantly and the regulators continued their strict application of the new appraisal standards, we could look to this "worst-case" scenario as becoming a real possibility. Under these circumstances we would continue to experience severe losses in amounts that could exceed the level of our capital. We could be essentially out of business.

Under the" most likely" scenario, which was the basis of our presentation, we could expect fewer loan loses, a gradual recovery, and a profitable year. As this scenario had been premised on a generally accepted improving economy and a more dubious softer regulatory environment, I was reasonably comfortable in using this relatively positive scenario as the basis of the presentation.

In the back of my mind and down deep, however, I wondered and worried just how realistic it was to expect a quick economic recovery and regulatory change. We had a lot riding on these assumptions. Was I presenting an honest view of the future? Was it unrealistic or should I have given them the "worst-case" scenario? I didn't think so.

ECONOMIC KNOWLEDGE– Business leaders should have a strong background in economic events and expectations to effectively judge the impact economic change might have on strategic thinking and direction.

ETHICAL – Business leaders should convey information applying strong ethical values, truthfulness, and honesty. The determination should be based on the leader's best individual assessment of the facts and assumptions relevant to the situation.

Somehow, the liquidity and funding crises of year end had not been seen as particularly relevant by the press or stock analysts as a compelling issue that might risk our future. Perhaps they just weren't aware of the full extent of the crisis; however, I was not intending to volunteer my experience in that matter. While we had resolved these issues, we had to look forward to rearranging our balance sheet and strategic thrust to ensure financial and liquidity stability along with meaningful earnings. This, we knew, would require that we had accounted for our troubles: consistent with "most likely" loss expectations, reduced regulatory tension and acceptance of a recovering positive economic forecast.

Following the presentation, I opened the floor to questions from those in attendance. As was typical in events involving these groups, many hands went up. We had recently become a point of interest for most of them, not only because of the reported difficulties but also because there had been a recent stream of rumors about the possibility of our combining with Well Fargo.

My San Francisco friend from the Chronicle had flown to New York for the meeting and was seated in the front row. I pointed to him to start the discussion.

"Have you had any meetings with Wells Fargo to discuss a possible combination of your banks?" he forcibly asked with a slight twist of his face knowing he had put me on the spot.

Remain as honest and forthright as you can, I said to myself.

"As you must expect we talk at various levels of our neighboring banks all the time, including the personal connections I have to many CEOs, including Wells." I responded. "We talk about a lot of things. But as you know, we are both long standing banking rivals who are committed to meeting the needs and expectations of our investor shareholders, employees, customers and the communities we serve. We are very different banks attempting to meet a variety of expectations through very different strategies. I don't think our interests and strategies blend well or are really compatible."

"But don't you think that such a combination would not only put the surviving bank among the three largest in the country, but it would also offer the investor shareholders and customers more in the way of confidence, especially during these difficult economic times. Wouldn't such a combination offer the capacity to become an earnings and banking service leader?"

"Sure, it could." I answered. "Maybe in the years ahead, but there is nothing that is in the works or is going to happen right now."

Another reporter chimed in with a more relevant question that made my legs begin to shake. Show no fear, I said to myself.

"How did you remain funded when you lost your top commercial paper rating?" he asked.

"With a lot of hard work on the part of some very key people," I responded.

"Did you talk to the Fed about the potential needs or the need to borrow from them?"

"We have continuing contact with the Fed, as you know, and they remain very cognizant of the risks we face. They remained very pleased with what we were doing. We were all pleased that our refunding came out very well. You know, we are much better off now, with considerably less short-term debt and a reduced level of risk. I am very pleased and confident of our future as we work through the economic difficulties," I said.

PERSUADING THE ANALYSTS

After about 45 minutes of questions from the press, I moved to meet with a small group of stock analysts and representatives of the debt rating agencies who tracked and routinely evaluated our company. The most relevant were the stock analysts, whose reports described the company and its earnings expectations and then advised their followers to either buy, hold, or sell the company's stock. By the nature of their work they look at the company's operating results and expectations from quarter to quarter, except that they also try to evaluate the expectations of acquisitions and mergers. With all that had gone on, we were clearly in their focus.

Over the past six months five of the analyst group who had previously recommended a stock buy of Security Pacific had changed their position to just holding the stock but not buying more or selling their ownership positions. With a loss reported for the past year following the announcement of the special charges, their primary concern was what the first quarter results might be. Unfortunately, because so much was dependent on future additions to the loan loss provision, I had no real idea of what those results might be. I was, however, seriously concerned about our reserve levels and the possibility that our results might show a loss for the quarter. I realized that this meeting should be handled very carefully so that they didn't move their recommendations farther away from holding our shares.

"What earnings do you expect for the first quarter?" An analyst who supported our company asked.

"We have, as you know, a great number of high cash flow producing activities that serve to mitigate the results of the troubled real estate loan portfolio. Our large branch network offers about $2 billion in pre-tax, pre-reserve cash flow per year and right now it is really humming. In addition, our non-bank financial services provide another half billion dollar in free cash flow. As we shut down the Merchant Bank we will continue to hold and benefit from many of its longstanding top earning activities. Other units, we believe, will be sold for considerable value as the function is disbanded. As you might already realize we are carefully analyzing our real estate loan portfolio, especially those project loans that are under development. This evaluation is a moving target, but we have always been conservative in our valuation of properties. However, the changes initiated through the new FIRREA appraisal requirements have impacted all our evaluations. We are processing those evaluations one at a time but look to our inherent strengths and the closure of the Merchant Bank as supportive of maintaining our earnings. The first quarter should be at least flat to last year."

"Will you experience other funding difficulties over the remainder of the year?"

"No, we have completed our refunding of the short-term items, and our retail and other unit cash flow should continue to be strong over the year," I responded. Overall, the difficulties we experienced in funding were a short-term event that was effectively managed. We have obviously extended much of our short-term financing well into the future. We are aggressively soliciting deposits and will be reducing our assets with the shut-down of the Merchant Bank. I don't think the funding difficulties could possibly recur."

"Will you merge with Wells?"

"We will consider anything that could enhance the shareholder value for our investors. There are currently restrictions that limit the opportunity of joining any bank headquartered outside of California. But we are very comfortable where we are. We have a broad network of retail and small business banking offices and other productive activities. This includes our network of finance companies as well as our extensive New York based processing operations. The restructuring of the Merchant Bank will eliminate many of the newer growth pieces that haven't adequately produced results, but we are retaining a number of our mature securities-related functions that are strong earners."

"Have the regulators put the bank under any of their classifications that limit your future or demand more capital, or have they made any comments about your personal future?"

"Well, you know I can't tell you what they have said, but as of now we are doing the right things to ensure compliance with their stated wishes. As for me personally, I remain serving at the direction and pleasure of the board of directors.

The discussion went on for about an hour, with several intense very pointed questions but overall, I concluded the discussion with the impression that we were still well regarded by most of the group.

In some respects that surprised me.

COMMUNICATIVE – It is important for business leaders to work closely in clearly and routinely communicating with all the constituents. Good communications should create a fair, clear, and understandable relationship between the leaders and these groups.

7

GETTING DOWN TO SIZE

THE MARTIN LUTHER KING DAY DEBACLE

In the years leading up to our troubles, the mask of successful banking was changing dramatically. We realized that the longstanding methods and models for successfully serving the customers, particularly consumers and small businesses, was in flux. The introduction of advancing technology and the move to centralize services was advancing rapidly. As a result of these changes, fewer activities were conducted by branch staff in the hours before and after the offices were open to the public. We saw the traditional banking model as needing significant change if we were to meet our strategic objectives of growth and increasing shareholder return.

It became clear that the less active periods each banking day could be better employed by opening the branch to public business beyond the traditional hours of 10 a.m. to a 3 p.m. closing. We also wanted to determine whether extending service on Saturday, Sunday, and certain holidays would be attractive to our customer base.

It seemed that we were open when the public was at work and did not serve them before or after work or when they might be available on the weekends. We were not benefiting from the moves we had made a few years earlier when we centrally consolidated various functions in the processing of deposits and checks as well as fulfilling requests for credit.

I called a meeting of my staff to discuss how we could make better use of our facilities and employees and increase the service period available to our customers. To this point in time, no other bank had yet explored extending its hours of service. As a result, we felt we had an opportunity to gain a marketing advantage over our competitors. The question was what impact such a change would have on our cost of conducting business and how much new business, if any, could we gain.

"I want to offer our clients additional hours in order to create an environment of easier access, better service, and as a result create an increased marketing opportunity," I opened the staff meeting saying.

"But that's why we are adding Automated Teller Machines," our branch senior officer noted.

"Yes, but that's a slow process that requires several years of customer assimilation in order to actually allow us to adjust our staff levels. In addition, forcing the customers outside does not permit us to effectively market new services or to open new accounts. It is only a low-cost access to cash and noncash deposits. While ATM transactions costs are about 10% of full teller transactions, we do lose customer contact. Until ATMs become more universally accepted and capable of offering a broader set of services, their utility for sales, customer contact, or financial discussions will remain somewhat limited."

FAIR – Business leaders should remain fair in balancing the many factors, situations, and interests inherent in their responsibilities to their staff, communities, investor shareholders, and customers.

"Wouldn't opening more hours require more staff costs?" our CFO asked.

"To your point, yes. Unless it is combined with a new model of service that employs staff that match the hours of customer demand. That is, if 50% of customer transactions are conducted during a couple of specific hours, then we will necessarily have to employ part-time employees to cover that period of demand. We certainly don't need full-time staff standing around with make-work waiting for the more active demand time window."

"Can we get capable staff on a part-time basis?" the CFO added.

"That's up to our Human Resources Officer or HRO, but I've heard that there are many mothers with young children who would love to work part time hours while their children are in school."

"I believe that's possible and could even improve the capability of our staff. They will be older, more mature and more focused on their hours of work and not trying to find ways to fill their day," our HRO noted. "We can pay them a higher hourly rate for their work because they would not qualify for health care and other benefits. This would save us those costs that we can partially pass on to them in higher hourly wages."

Our branch head then chimed in to add, "I have thought a lot about this possibility and know it will take some time to fully implement and more than likely even cause a bit of stress among some of our branch personnel. This is a dramatic change in our business model and I am assuming that we can hire and train the right people to service the customers. I know that after a few months we can accurately project the appropriate hour-by-hour staffing to fully service our customer needs at the lowest possible cost."

After a pause, while he shuffled through his papers, he continued. "I am going to propose that we open our branches at 9 a.m. instead of the traditional 10 a.m. opening and that we stay open until 5 p.m., two hours beyond the longstanding 3 p.m. close. We will continue to remain open to 6 p.m. on Fridays. Keep in mind that much of the pre- and post-opening work is now done at processing centers. We will put the full-time people to work serving customers in periods outside of the high activity hours. The busiest hours, depending on demand expectations, will be supplemented by part-time workers. I would also propose that we open Saturdays and many nonsignificant holidays from 9 a.m. to 2 p.m."

"We will have to price this out before we start," our CFO noted.

"Of course, we will do the best we can, but I don't think we have any other choice. We have to step up on this one and make it work. We must staff according to need and demand rather than having a group who works all day, sometimes with a lot of activity and other hours with little to do. The customers are the ones who will benefit, and every other bank will be under pressure to do the same thing," I noted.

"What about the holidays?" our HRO noted. "Which ones are in and which are out?"

"Well the major holidays we will close, but we should open on President's Day, Columbus Day, and I would suggest the new Martin Luther King Day. "

We spent the next six months planning and modifying our staff hours as well as hiring and training over 500 part-time employees. It was all thought through carefully, and in November we made a public announcement of the changes. The press reports were positive while the stock analysts, concerned about the impact on earnings, were suspicious. On January 2nd, we implement the changes with strong customer praise and continuing press positives.

> COLLABORATIVE - It is important that business leaders work in collaboration with all personnel and groups to achieve workable and acceptable decisions. Collaborative thinking includes the ability to compromise on issues and actions to satisfy the interests of the included groups and the company.

Everything went well until Monday January 16th, Martin Luther King Day and the first holiday that we had decided to open from 9 a.m. to 2 p.m., the same hours that we would open on Saturday. We expected little trouble but realized that we operated twenty-nine offices in the predominantly African American communities in South-Central Los Angeles and Watts. We had concluded that this change should be perceived as a positive action to the local community intended to provide them an opportunity to conduct business at times apart from the normal work week.

We went to the office that day with positive thoughts. It was about 9:10 a.m. when the first phone rang followed quickly by a constant barrage of residents of the South-Central community and city officials. Each were calling to object to our failure to respect the honor intended for Martin Luther King on his first national holiday. Then came more calls, including threats of bombs, riots, and burning down the branches. No explanation or rational discussion worked. We had disrespected the leader of the black community and would pay for our actions. At about 10:30 a.m. after alerting our security people but not wanting to start World War III, I told the administrator to advise all of the branches in the area to politely but quickly close for the day and to apologize to the community leaders, assuring them we would not make the same mistake in the following years.

While we did not anticipate that our actions would cause this disturbance on Martin Luther King Day in the African American community, the overall program acceptance was exceptional. Over the months account growth exceeded the prior years by a substantial margin, with deposit and loan growth far exceeding our expectation. Most importantly, with the introduction of part-time employees, overall staff costs dropped and our new service efficiency was highly praised in customer surveys.

The results were positive for the bank, but in the effort to move quickly ahead with this strategy we had lacked the thoroughness of a detailed and well thought out plan. We had failed to fully consider the impact of this decision on a very important part of our community. We had not been disciplined enough to consult with members of the African American areas of the city with respect to the relevance and significance of this new holiday and the memory of Dr. King.

> *DISCIPLINED – Remaining disciplined when considering new strategies or changes to historical processes and traditions is an important leadership aspect.*

MERGING FROM WITHIN

As the benefits of technology advanced, ATMs access grew, operations centralized, and our service hours extended, we were not yet able to realize a positive changes to our bottom-line. We needed to find means to make our large network of branch offices a growing source of earnings to the company.

By early 1990 the total retail and small business branch offices of Security Pacific consisted of over one thousand throughout the seven Western states. The expansion to neighboring states had been accomplished under permissible regional compacts that circumvented the restrictive provisions of the McFadden Act. The branches remained the core of the bank's one-hundred-and-twenty-year history dating back to 1871, when the first office opened as Farmers and Merchants Bank in Southern California. At that time, the population of the city was about 7,000 persons, most of whom had migrated to sunny Southern California from all parts of the United States.

I called a meeting of my staff to explore how we could gain more value from our investments in technology and the changed operations of the branch offices.

"We have branches on nearly every other street corner in most of the urban areas. There aren't many areas that we don't cover in the Western states, yet our earnings from this activity remain strong, yet flat, I advanced as an opening comment.

"Yes, and they all do very well. We have over $100 million in deposits in many of these locations and collectively I believe we are doing a great job of serving our customers. But we do need to get a better return on this investment," our head of retail banking noted.

He continued, "maybe we should just find ways to improve our advertising and marketing to grow these offices faster. They can all handle more customers without adding staff. In addition, let's not forget that a growing portion of our customer service is now accomplished through our ATM network as well as more and more drive-up windows. We are also doing a great job in servicing our clients more conveniently with our extended hours," he added. But in this process we have given up the advantage of meeting with customers and selling more services through in-branch contact. Many of our customers are faceless to us.

PATIENT - In an effort to preserve the ongoing success of the business, it is important that business leaders respond to matters of change while remaining cautious and patient.

At that point, the senior officer of our finance companies made a very interesting and sensible point to move our thinking forward. "I don't know too much about this entire operation, but what significance is there in offering service to customers within a few blocks of the next available service location? Since many clients use ATMs and most drive to their branch offices, what risk is there in asking them to travel a few more blocks to another nearby location? If we accepted that premise, we could consolidate many branch offices, reduce redundant staff, lower costs, and I'll bet not lose many accounts."

"To add to that thought, I have become aware that a growing number of customers don't even go into the branch anymore. They are becoming more and more aware that they can access any of our growing number of ATMs, utilize their home computers for account information, or just use the mail." I added.

"But many customers love the community nature of their branch office and their favorite tellers and other officers. These are generally older clients who see the branch as a social center," the branch leader said.

"Yes, and on the other side are the younger more business-oriented customers who want convenience, speed, and lower costs; I think we can serve both. The potential to reduce operating costs at the branch level by merging local offices would be significant," I added.

"Won't this mean that we would be laying off or displacing hundreds of our twelve thousand branch employees, including managers, supervisors, and other officers?" our HRO commented. "We will have to develop a plan to provide a soft landing for these people as well as a methodology to fairly determine who we retain and which employees get displaced."

COMPASSIONATE – *It is important that business leaders fairly equate and balance with compassion and understanding the social and work impact of decisions and actions on employees and customers.*

A plan was developed to implement a test area to consolidate branches within defined criteria, including the physical premises, available entry routes, parking, community needs, terms of lease or ownership, and other factors. Six months following the implementation of the consolidation of about a quarter of the branches in the test area, we discovered that we had eliminated 90% of the combined branch operating costs and staff expenses and maintained 95% of the combined deposit account customers.

When the plan was implemented over a two-year period throughout the entire network of branches, the bottom line earnings of all our retail and small business banking operations increased by over 50%.

8

FOCUSING ON THE EMPLOYEES

IT WAS A WHITE MALE WORLD

T hroughout most of this early period, we could best be described as a bank of predominantly white males. Like most businesses, we had an Affirmative Action program directed at increasing our complement of women and minorities, particularly African Americans and to a lesser degree Hispanics and Asians. While tellers and other lesser positions were easily filled to meet our plan objective, it was difficult to find and attract qualified, college-trained minorities to our officer positions. There was considerably more demand than there was supply of college-trained female and minority candidates and as a result, we were continually falling short in meeting our goals to expand the female and minority presence of officers

Additionally, when meaningful officer positions opened, it was rare that a female or minority would be included on the prospect list. In other words, the traditional white males were reluctant to include those whom they didn't know or whom they didn't yet have a close affiliation. The white males wanted to maintain control of the process for themselves and their close male friends.

While most of the team openly expressed a commitment to our Affirmative Action Plan, few gave it more than a smile and a nod. They all talked the game, but when it came down to hiring or promoting a female or minority, the excuses for exclusion remained the same; They are not qualified; they don't have the background or experience; they are not as well educated at a top university. Often the excuses were more severe; they won't be respected; their subordinates will be smarter; the customers won't like it; I'm too dependent on my trained staff to take a chance.

I heard argument after argument on these subjects and often openly called out subordinates who did not reflect the necessary commitment to expand the presence of women and minorities among our officers and more senior leaders. I felt I was fighting an uphill battle to implement both the words and spirit of our plan.

I called my staff together to discuss how we could better manage this process. My staff, at that time, consisted of six white males; none were minorities, and one woman who was a lawyer designated as our Corporate Secretary. This was not a particularly meaningful or respected position compared to our CFO, CCO, Chief Technology Officer, Head of Retail Banking, Head of Human Resources, and so forth.

"What can we do to hire and promote more women and minorities to bank officers and more senior executive positions?" I asked.

"I'm not sure they are there to hire," our HRO said. "We can't get the better ones to join us. Perhaps that is because they don't see us as welcoming as others."

"Let's pay them more," said the head of Retail Banking.

"More than the white males?" I asked.

"Well, let's make it more attractive for everyone."

"Gee, I think we have done pretty well," The Chief Technology Officer noted.

"Really," I said. How many women and minority officers do you have on your staff?"

"Hmm," he stammered, "Most of them don't have the qualifications or background."

"Why don't you hire them and give them the training?" I asked.

"I guess we could do that. But that will cost us a bundle."

It was obvious that this was not a subject that evoked much enthusiasm. It seemed that their interest was limited to getting by and doing only the minimum required.

Then out of nowhere the only female on my staff spoke. "I think that none of you are carrying out your corporate as well as human responsibilities to establish a welcoming environment of fairness. If a woman, as I am, or minority heard this conversation, why would they want to come to work for Security Pacific? They would quickly recognize that we do not promote opportunity for all. We don't want to change and will do whatever it takes to keep the good old boys together, without any female or minority intrusion, for as long as we can. We are not meeting our responsibilities as bank officers and frankly as good human beings."

COMPASSIONATE – Business leaders should reflect a welcoming compassion for all persons. They should accept and promote with sound judgement and equality avoiding any form of bias or discrimination in their decisions, actions and communication.

SELECTIVE – Business leaders should be selective in accepting the most qualified candidates for employment and promotion. However, to meet social and legal expectations and obligations, they must, at times, deviate from this practice in order to maintain an ethnically and diverse work force.

There was a prolonged period of silence. She had spoken the truth and wanted us to change. I knew she was a devoted progressive liberal, but I did not know she would be a champion and advocate for the cause of equality in business. I had never thought of her as an outspoken advocate for anything and was truly impressed with her thoughts and comments

The following month I made several staff changes but the most important was to promote my sole female staff member, who served as Corporate Secretary as the HRO, with one specific charge. "Get us compliant with Affirmative Action and change the attitude of my staff and other officers in order to bring about change. Also, adjust our training, pay and promotion policies to ensure that women and minorities are adequately prepared for more senior positions as well as fairly compensated and adequately reflected in our senior staffing within the next five years."

While we continued to struggle with these issues, she made considerable progress in increasing the complement and promotion of women and minorities. She was less successful, however, in altering the minds of many of our white-male officers. They went along with her leadership because they knew they had to. At the end of our time at Security Pacific she had performed so well that she was selected to lead Bank of American's HR function following our merger.

REFOCUSING THE STAFF

Beginning in the months immediately following the announcement of the special year-end charges, the employee group began to develop a different attitude toward fulfilling their job expectations. They were making maximum of use of sick days, early use of vacation time, and a reluctance to turn in work assignments on time. It was reasonable that the general work force felt at risk about their potential job growth within the organization and what might be in store, overall, for them individually. Their attitude toward their jobs changed, and an increasing portion of each day was spent talking over the water cooler about the impact of change and our financial decline, gossiping about rumors and speculating about what might happen to the company. Overall productivity declined, but most importantly was each employee's concern for his or her own career.

I knew that one of the key elements of our eventual survival and recovery during some questionable times ahead was to be able to maintain the momentum and cash flow of our retail banking activities. These activities included our one thousand plus retail banking offices that served our five million plus retail clients and a million plus small business clients in our multi-state service area.

I called a meeting of my staff to discuss strategies and actions that could help ensure that we maintained this strong cash flow from the branch group.

"What can we do to keep our better staff and to ensure that the staff focus remains on their responsibilities? We want to be sure the group continues to generate strong earnings that are an important element ot the company as we work through our credit difficulties," I stated.

"I think they will keep doing what they have been doing so well. I don't think any special action will be necessary. They are all committed people who are very loyal to Security Pacific," out HRO noted.

"But their loyalty ceases when they see their own futures becoming uncertain or in jeopardy," I responded.

"I am concerned that we can keep their attention to the business at hand," the branch group head commented. "And if we don't do something, we will lose business and many capable employees. Keep in mind that our own customer base has also been shocked by this situation and many are concerned that their bank has shown weaknesses that may put the bank and their relationship in jeopardy."

"So, what do you suggest?" I asked. "You know, all of this is something none of our branch office employees had anything to do with. They didn't make the real estate loans or conceptualize the Merchant Bank. They didn't pass new restrictive laws; they just kept improving our retail and small business system of branches. Now they are suffering under the uncertainty of a troubled bank. I think we have to do everything we can to put them at ease and give them the comfort to know they are doing a good job and contributing to the results of the bank."

The banking office head responded. "I think that we should give them the comfort of knowing that their jobs are secure for some time. Most the them, especially the longer tenured employees, should be made to feel that their jobs are safe, perhaps for a couple of years, and those at a more senior and important level should be offered a retention bonus. If they remain and continue to perform their jobs over the next six to nine months and hopefully during the few months required to get our troubles out of the way, they should receive added compensation. Additionally, I believe that for the average worker, we should create a sales program with results-oriented competitions. We should structure the program to include rewards for sales, all intended to take their mind away from our troubles, allowing them to focus on their jobs. We want to get them away from the water cooler conversations and rumors and motivate them to focus on new business and serving the existing clients well. We'll reward the winners with trips and prizes for their results, making sure there are lots of winners."

"I'm not sure what the total cost will be, but the alternatives are unacceptable. Let's do everything we can to keep our employees and their customers relationships strong. Really the costs won't matter if we can keep the earnings coming in. Put together your plan and let's get it implemented over the next couple of weeks."

DECISIVE – In certain situations, business leaders should be willing to take quick decisive action based upon their experience, expected impact, personal intuition, and the implications of delay.

COMPASSIONATE – It is important for business leaders to be considerate and understanding of the needs, concerns, and feelings of company employees and customers. Leadership should take whatever actions are necessary to minimize the impact of troubled times and situations that impact the staff and all related groups.

Both the retention and sales programs were developed with the help of outside consultants who were experienced in staff motivation. The success of these two programs was exceptional. Generally, employees felt more secure and gained greater confidence in their sales and service capabilities, and at the same time found the security of a guaranteed reward commitment. Many enjoyed their trip to Hawaii or a new big-screen TV. We considered these rewards as a better option than cash, which leaves no memory, is invisible to others, and is fungible to a family's finances. The employees gradually moved away from the water cooler.

In addition to the employee programs, we began a weekly newsletter that kept the staff up to date on the results of employee programs as well as the progress the bank was making in shutting down the Merchant Bank and more clearly identifying the real estate loan problems. We openly announced our activities and actions, even though we knew that much of this information would be picked up by the press and others in the outside world. We were carefully putting our troubles in the open on the basis that we had nothing to hide. In this way we were able to convey the information in terms we found acceptable, which were superior to relying on the rumor mill or depending on the interpretation of reporters, many of whom were not our fans.

STRESS TAKES ITS TOLL

Several weeks after the commercial paper funding crisis and the effort to regain funding stability, my long standing Chief Credit Officer staggered lethargically into my office, his head down and near tears. "I basically can't handle it anymore. The problems are too severe," he said.

"What are you telling me?"

"I'm going home. Please don't call."

That was it. he turned slowly — the way a wrecking ball changes direction—and walked out.

FEARLESS – It is necessary that business leaders respond to negative circumstances or situations without expressing or indicating personal fears, both publicly or directly to their staff or related groups.

He appeared to be having some sort of meltdown. I knew in the past months he'd suffered through onerous disagreements about credit requests with one of our key executives. But what else might be going on? I wondered.

Some of the prophetic words he'd spoken at the Hawaii American Bankers Association conference and our recent management forum echoed now in my mind: ". . . during a period of economic downturn and possibly even more important from a risk-management perspective, in the months preceding an economic downturn, the issue of asset quality becomes a dominant factor affecting the company's performance. Today, in my judgment, we're witnessing a very classic pattern. The warning signs are now clearly evident."

He probably felt like a lone voice crying out in the wilderness.

I was enormously sympathetic toward him because he was an extraordinary person who had done a lot for Security Pacific; by the same token, the fact that he had simply called it quits scared the hell out of me. He was our Chief Credit Officer — my God, were things this desperate? What did he know about our credit situation that I didn't know? Was it even worse than we suspected? Was he just getting in the lifeboat before the Titanic sank? How could it be?

I hurried to my HRO's office. "You're not going to believe this. As if we haven't got enough problems, our CCO just went home. He's totally upset. He nearly collapsed in my office."

"You mean he just walked? Will he come back?"

"Damned if I know."

"I'm worried that this might be the straw that breaks the camel's back?"

"Well, this is just awful, look at 1990. Look at the quarter. The last two months of the year have been positively hellish. The Wells deal collapsed, bad loans are skyrocketing, we have a funding crisis, we've lost 15% of our capital with the redemption of the preferred stock, we've lost our prime commercial paper rating, and now the credit agencies are threatening to downgrade our long-term debt. He probably just saw a couple of new loans go bad and absolutely couldn't stand it anymore."

"You know, every man has a breaking point."

Two weeks later, our CCO had still not returned to work. I called two already over-extended executives to pick up the slack in his absence.

If our lending apparatus had a systemic weakness, it was likely the result of our emphasis on growth. Because growth became a function of the number rather than the quality of loans, no one wanted to say no. No one wanted to be the messenger who issued a caution that resulted in increased losses and reserves. We'd prided ourselves in growth and frowned upon any gesture that restrained it. We'd built an inherent paradox: if we'd stopped lending, our earnings would have been less impressive and our board might have called for a scalp or two. But if we kept going until the bottom fell out, there would also have been calls for a scalp. The CCO was damned either way. Something had to give.

Following an anguishing period, he returned to work several weeks later. He looked great, but I couldn't place him back in his prior position.

He needed to be out of the credit approval loop. Unfortunately, word had spread about what had happened.

At the next board meeting held at San Diego's Hotel Del Coronado, our senior board member asked me to join him for a stroll around the bay. Never one to mince words, he began what I thought would be a casual discussion by saying, "The credit is going from bad to worse and you can't have your CCO walking out of the building. I think that he succumbed to pressure from another executive to extend credit in cases where it was not advisable to do so."

"He has already admitted that he had yielded to pressure on some credits that he didn't really like." I was torn; I didn't entirely blame him, but I was also pissed that others had applied a jackhammer to him. "He was overwhelmed."

"That may be true, but I think you should get rid of him." This was not the first time this director had issued such proclamations. A year earlier he'd wanted me to axe an employee for not pulling our Arizona interests out of the quagmire more quickly. I had refused him then and would do so now.

"No way, I need him. I won't fire him. He won't make credit decisions for this company anymore, but I need him because not only is he an excellent credit administrator, he knows the inner mechanisms of the portfolio. He lives and breathes this stuff, and he knows the condition and status of all our major loans. I depend on him for his knowledge of individual loans, especially right now. Cutting him loose would be stupid."

Our director was upset. "Somebody's got to take responsibility for this."

ACCOUNTABLE – Business leaders should stand fully accountable for the company's actions and results, including the impact resulting from troubling situations.

"I'm not going to get rid of him," I repeated. "He's a good banker and he would never do anything intentionally to harm Security Pacific. Firing him is not in the best interest of this company." If you want the responsible party, blame me. Fire me, if that will make you happy."

He winced and said nothing more. It was a long walk back to the hotel.

COMPASSIONATE – Business leaders should display compassion and understanding of circumstances in situations impacting their staff.

Following this meeting, I assigned our vanishing CCO as the overall administrator of the existing credit portfolio without any credit approval responsibilities.

SELECTIVE - It is important that business leaders be fair and reasoned judges and be selective in obtaining and assigning the best and most qualified staff that meets the collective needs of the company.

GETTING RID OF A KEY EXECUTIVE

About nine months after I had assumed the CEO role in January 1990, I was beginning to personally absorb the stress of failing loans and a poorly performing Merchant Banking operation. At this time, I was also in early discussions with Wells about a possible merger of our two banks. I was talking with my wife over a dinner at a local restaurant about many of the more positive as well as negative aspects of my new job. While she had noticed that my mood had not been very positive over the past few months, she was nevertheless trying to ease my stress by talking positively about the new position and the accomplishments I had garnered in my nearly thirty-year career.

After we enjoyed some laughter and a pre-dinner cocktail, her smile seemed to diminish as she spoke. "Notwithstanding your efforts and accomplishments so far, I have to talk to you about a serious problem you have at the bank."

"My God," I thought, how does she know that so many of our real estate loans are turning sour, with no immediate fix in sight? Is she aware of a specific failing project? Does she think or has she heard rumor that I was fooling around with a teller?

She then went on. "I think that you've become too engaged and blind in supporting your senior head of the Merchant Bank. While I don't have a strong opinion, one way or the other, I hear nothing but negative comments from his reporting officers and many of their wives. They see him as a narcissist who denigrates his employees with insults about their jobs and leadership qualities. They generally hate him and see him as a negative element in your leadership, considering your continued support of his actions. In essence, he is tearing you down. You complain about the weak performance of the Merchant Bank and yet have never spoken about his lack of management and leadership as the cause of these weak results."

She paused, and I stayed quiet to hear her out.

She went on. "He is an albatross around your neck and perhaps is the cause of some of your stress."

Then she really came clean to advise me on my leadership. "I think you have to get rid to this guy and that will help you survive these troubled times."

Unfortunately, while I didn't like her sticking her nose in what I felt was my business alone, I trusted her common sense and "people feel" qualities and most of all her guts in telling me exactly how she felt. I was not yet convinced but knew that I must listen and learn about things that perhaps I was unaware of or in part had heard but just didn't want to believe. I saw many of the same character traits she noted, but I had become solely dependent on his strong technical qualities, his knowledge of all aspects of the Merchant Bank, and his demonstrated ability to work through tough, challenging times. I had ignored the personal flaws plus the insulting demeanor he had shown on many occasions.

SELECTIVE - Business leaders are expected to judge and select the best most qualified team to meet the needs of the company. Thoroughness and depth of examination are critical elements of this process.

In addition, I had no one on staff who could replace him in his capacity as the head of the Merchant Bank. I wondered if negative personal characteristics and attitude really overcame the need for his technical knowledge and his part in developing the Merchant Bank. I knew I couldn't personally run both the bank and the Merchant Banking activities. To replace him from outside the company would require at least six months, and I was cognizant that I had been thinking about scrapping the whole thing. I had listened and now I wanted time the think hard about what had been said. I also wanted to talk to a few of my trusted staff about their impressions of his leadership and staff reputation.

I had become unwilling to effectively deal with the negative implications and impact of a person whose leadership qualities failed to support the human needs of the employees. In not acting, I was communicating my acceptance of his poor leadership to other members of the staff.

COMMUNICATIVE – Business leaders should be willing to listen and fairly consider the thoughts of their staff.

DECISIVE - It is important for business leaders to take timely decisive action to remove disruptive persons.

Over the next couple of weeks, I had private discussions with my HRO and Chief Legal Counsel, plus a couple of leading directors who had strong connections with many of our leadership team. They all seemed less aware of the shortcomings and his impact on the employees and felt that his loss at this time would just put greater stress on the entire operation and specifically on me. They also felt that because of the customer nature of many of his functions, his loss might result in a staff exodus in some areas and the corresponding loss of customers that would impact the unit's income.

The final decision to let him go was made two months later, when I finalized my plan to shut down the Merchant Bank. I had held on to him for a couple of months following the discussion with my wife but took her thoughts to heart when making the decision to shutter his activities.

9

BUILDING THE COMPANY

FINDING NEW REVENUE OPPORTUNITIES

T en years prior to our troubles, under new leadership at the start of a new decade Security Pacific embarked on a strategy of growth, growth, and more growth. The world of banking was changing as more and more competitors, including many non–bank financially-related entities were creating new ways to attract customers to new products and services. New concepts using technology that offered customers more convenience with greater returns at less cost were rapidly growing.

Credit cards were promoted as an easy credit opportunity by banks as well as retail merchants that had gained access to the bank clearing systems. Auto dealers were actively offering financing, which allowed them to package sales pricing with financing. Most broker dealers were offering trust and investment services plus access to personal credit as well as deposit and card products and services. Each day more and more non–bank financial companies wanted to attract consumers, especially high-income persons with accumulated wealth.

No longer did banks have control or dominance in the traditional form of deposit taking, investment, and lending. Savings and loan, brokers, credit unions, mutual funds, insurance companies, and other financial service companies were chasing and gaining traditional bank customers. It was clear that to maintain customer control with strong asset and earnings growth, banks had to find new ways to expand their products and services.

An additional early effort to overcome the growing threat to the traditional banking business was initiated at Security Pacific in the late 1970s. We began expanding our banking offices and activities both nationally and internationally. In addition, we began to expand our activities away from banking in higher risk consumer and commercial finance companies and leasing activities. We also formed a small business investment company and began offering different forms of specialized equipment and home financing. These new companies, operated as subsidiaries of our holding company, initiated fixed-rate assets funded by the issuance of top grade low-cost short-term commercial paper. This funding was to later become the center of our liquidity troubles. We had for years operated these companies with extreme caution but had later initiated more aggressive risk and leverage policies intended to maximize growth and profits.

PROTECTIVE – Business leaders should be protective of the company in balancing the risk and return expectations of decisions and actions as well as investments intended to meet the company's objectives.

We had also initiated an international business activity in the mid-1970s focused on extending credit in the developing countries, specifically in Mexico and Central and South America. By the mid-1980s, this higher-risk international business strategy was experiencing serious difficulties as the Mexico, Central and South American developing countries and their major businesses defaulted on most of their bank obligations. The resolution of these troubles amounted to over $100 billion in banking industry write-offs over a five-year period and cost Security Pacific over $2 billion during that same period.

During the decade of the 1980s, the entire savings and loan industry was going through prolonged troubles, leading up to its eventual collapse by the end of that period. In this environment, we felt it opportunistic to explore other newer markets, products, and services in order to achieve our intended level of growth.

By the mid-1980s the federal regulations prohibiting the expansion of our banking services to consumers beyond our state had changed as more and more states acted to permit interstate growth by utilizing the lawfulness of interstate compacts. This change allowed the possibility for market growth through the acquisition of banks in neighboring states. When California acted, the change offered strong strategic incentives for Security Pacific, with expansion through acquisitions in Arizona, Nevada, Oregon, and Washington.

In this same period, we felt there was a strong possibility of changes to the Glass-Stegall Act, which for five decades had prohibited banks from expanding their services into many aspects of the securities business. We believed that we understood these markets, and growth in this area offered a unique opportunity.

CREATIVE – Business leaders should seek opportunities to expand business through new markets, products, and services. This is especially attractive when early participation in a new or expanded market would be preemptive or unique within the industry.

FEARLESS – Seeking new opportunities and fearlessly developing positive plans structured to minimize risk while benefitting from new and expanded markets and revenue are important to business leaders.

While interstate banking expansion was an obvious growth opportunity, we also looked to the potential expansion in the securities business as a real priority, even without the anticipated legislative changes to Glass-Stegall. Two early discoveries opened the door for our early participation in the securities business. First, we discovered that with a broker partner we could offer our customers a full plate of mutual funds and discount brokerage services (stock brokerage without offering advice). Second, we found that this restrictive banking legislation limiting securities activities did not prohibit a full array of equity underwriting and distributing activities in countries outside of the United States.

I called my staff together to explore how we could initially expand our consumer offerings to our five million branch customers. We wanted to explore the opportunities offered by providing mutual funds and discount brokerage services. Both areas were part of our focus on pre-empting other banks before any formal changes were made to Glass-Stegall.

"How can we possibly get the critical mass of customers needed to afford the infrastructure required to build a discount brokerage operation?" the CFO asked. "I think we can expect to eat losses for several years, as I'm sure it will be a slow process of converting our customers to our broker."

"Your point is valid, but to bypass those costs I've had discussions with Fidelity Brokerage Services and they are willing to provide back office support for our customers. While their participation will cut into the transaction margins, with sufficient volume we can make this business profitable much faster than going it alone. In addition, we will gain better control of our customers and probably gain some new clients in the process. It's going to be a real challenge to make money, but over the long term it will be something we will need. You know that we tried to buy Charles Schwab, but Bank of America beat us out by paying twice our offer. There are many other discount brokers, but Schwab is the leader. My idea is to accumulate several smaller discount brokerage operations, each of which has a customer base, and switch them all to the Fidelity back office. At the same time, we will work to convert our branch clients to use our brokerage operation for their stock and bond activities," I responded.

"Makes sense, but this venture will not be any quick source of new revenues; however, any new income source that grows our customer relationship should be positive to us in the long run," our head of retail banking noted.

After discussing other new service and market ideas, including establishing an insurance brokerage and income tax preparation service, our focus turned to the idea of establishing proprietary mutual funds to offer as an investment opportunity to our branch customers.

"Won't such a move reduce the level of low-cost deposits held by our branches, thereby raising the cost of funding? I realize that we would collect fees for managing the investments, but won't we also need an underwriting partner, like Fidelity, who will take their share of the fees? I think we will not gain but lose earnings," our branch head noted.

"That's all true but aren't those same deposits leaving the bank anyway? Right now, many of our customers are moving their accounts to other fund managers or securities companies," I responded. "I think we have to be in the business to hold onto the customers and to keep them in our family, utilizing our loans, investment, trust services, and other offerings. We have to stay up with all bank and non-bank competitors in this fast-changing financial world."

The initiation of both a discount brokerage operation and proprietary mutual funds was an excruciating experience, even with the assistance of Fidelity. While earnings were slow in materializing, both operations were helpful in building more client relationships and in establishing us as a banking leader in the development of new earnings opportunities and services for our customers.

By the mid-1980's we initiated entry into other aspects of the securities business. These areas began as a growth and earnings opportunity related to the operation function associated with the bank's trust activities. This opportunity would ultimately become part of the Merchant Bank.

For years the trust group had lost money focused on handling wills, estate probates, and testamentary trusts and serving as custodian of large blocks of securities and investments. These were all supplemented by operating a poorly performing investment management activity. It was an inefficient old school effort to accommodate the fiduciary and investment needs of older customers.

One of our early hires to a weakly preforming and stodgy Trust Department introduced us to potentially investing in a New York based securities custody and processing business that was serving primarily institutional clients. Looking for new revenue opportunities for the lethargic trust group, he introduced us to a team of five, all of whom had spent their careers on Wall Street dealing with the processing, clearing, and custody of securities. Looking for such new opportunity we agreed to employ them, paying a small bonus for their existing small book of clearing and custody business.

Fast forwarding this beginning our growth was dramatic, resulting primarily from the expansion into new products and services through a few small acquisitions. We were acting as custodian, processing and brokering several forms of government and private debt securities for a growing number of Wall Street clients. We also had started a repo/reverse repo or government securities financing operation and were serving as a processing trustee of a new growing mortgage-backed securities business. Many of these areas were new but turned out to be non-asset or capital-intensive activities providing strong returns to the bank. By the end of the decade, this group of businesses was contributing after-tax profits of over $150 million dollars a year to the bank.

Given our early background in the securities business and a belief that regulations restricting bank securities activities in the U.S. would soon end, our minds turned to foreign-based securities and related activities in which we could underwrite and distribute securities.

"Do you really think that we have sufficient knowledge to enter new securities-related markets without assuming significantly greater risk?" I asked the head of the Merchant Bank.

"Yes, but I would only do so by acquiring selected franchises with trusted and skilled operating experts," he responded. "I think that the most mature markets outside of the U.S. are in the English-speaking countries. Let's start in England, Canada, and Australia before we move into Germany or France. Building upon our existing New York operations while entering the equity markets through London as the financial capital in Europe, I think we can successfully manage these efforts and make a lot of money. I already have some names of respected companies and top performing executives in each of these markets."

"That sounds challenging, and I am convinced that we must set ourselves up for a changing world," I responded. "I think we will have a leg up on the competition and can perhaps start making up for lost business that has, for years, been moving to the growing non–bank financial services companies. These companies have, for at least ten years, been drawing clients from our traditional business and the most profitable markets," I noted. "These securities-related areas should be the cornerstone of strategic thinking over the next few years.

The head of the Merchant Bank continued, "at the same time, I think we can take advantage of our customer base by building out the newer growth markets, particularly interest rate and foreign currency swaps. These areas provide big margins, and we have been able to attract interest from some of the best people to work with us in these areas. As these hedging products expand, the breadth and competitive attraction of our corporate lending business should grow significantly."

The companies that were formed and accumulated over the three following years became the cornerstones of our later underperforming and disbanded Merchant Bank.

ENTERTAINING THE REAL ESTATE MOGULS

During the years leading up to our difficulties, we had proved to be very successful in developing and holding onto the top real estate developers in many parts of the country. While our clients were heavily weighted to companies headquartered in California and Arizona, many of them had large development interests in other parts of the country. Our success was in part due to our efforts in marketing and promoting ourselves as the banking leader in meeting the needs of the biggest and best real estate development companies. As a result of our special interest in this group, we tried to find special ways to entertain these industry leaders, providing them with experiences that they would consider special and hold in their memories.

The largest part of our business was focused on home building, resort and mixed-use project developers. We had nine-figure loans outstanding to many of these industry leaders, who looked to us for the money to leverage their capital in land and building developments.

They all wanted us as their banker, and we wanted them as well in the hope that our partnership would bring us both strong returns for our participation. One inherent problem was that the developer would earn a profit on their invested capital while we were limited to interest on the loan even though we often held a greater share of the risk. Typically, we would lend about three dollars for every dollar of their investment. In some cases, we would offer them unsecured lines of credit that I was sure were used to meet their capital needs. In other words, we could account for up to 100% of a project's total investment.

In our effort to insure our continued involvement with the industry leaders, ahead of Wells Fargo or Bank of American, we typically organized our annual sales and marketing event early in the year. Our third annual meeting was structured around conveying to the developers our continuing involvement, knowledge and commitment to the industry.

These affairs, were held in early Spring at the Vintage Club located in Indian Wells California, just up the road from historic Palm Springs. The events included gourmet dinners by renowned chefs, special selected wines, two days of golf, and top speakers on business, the economy and golf. This year, in addition to our Chief Economist, who presenting an optimist yet cautious outlook for the year ahead, we were joined by career grand slam champion Gary Player. He joined us in golf with our best customers and talked before dinner about his life and the need to maintain positive thinking in golf as well as business and life. He, of course, received a significant stipend for his words.

> *CREATIVE – Business leaders should seek creative means to connect the company to its most important customers.*

In good years these events were true brag fests with stories of successes and exceptional profits running throughout most of the conversations. Typically, there would be about sixty attendees, including nearly all the industry giants. All of the attendees were our customers, with whom we wanted to continue as the lead banker.

The Vintage founder was one of our attendees, and over half of those in attendance had a villa or home at this world recognized club. Most of the club members, who wanted to outdo their friends, sought to develop bigger and more expensive homes at the Vintage than their contemporaries. A few were joined by their second or third wives who were typically blond, gorgeous, and in their 30s. One developer, in particular, went so far as to be joined by his two young female friends who participated in his after-golf cocktail party held at his multi-million-mansion situated on the top of a small hill overlooking the entire course. My best guess was that the girls were for his personal use; at least that is what he told me before we teed-off on the first hole the next day. He said he was really tired after a night in the hot tub and that was the reason he wasn't playing very well.

During our gatherings the ladies spent their time shopping at the nearby boutiques, traveling back and forth in their Rolls Royce's or Ferrari's. They spent the afternoons lying by the pool and dashing in and out of the Spa. With no female developers in our group and the wives and their friends at the shops, club, pool, or spa, the events were full of booze, late nights, and rough locker-room talk.

We all found time, however, to remain committed to grow our businesses and profits, hoping that California and its historically near-perfect economy would allow that to happen for many years ahead. Little did we know how dramatically the events of the following year would alter our hopes and dreams. These annual events certainly left a lasting impression with the developers, but perhaps this particular year it was the wrong-one, since our deal-flow continued while the economy was collapsing.

PUSHING THE ENVELOPE

In mid-decade we embarked on buying, selling, and managing a variety of securities-related businesses that included New York–based brokering operations. These ventures all became part of the later disbanded Merchant Banking operation. We began with the acquisition of RMJ Securities, a U.S. securities broker populated by a number of money driven young hotshots, This wild bunch served as brokers for undisclosed Wall Street securities firms in the purchase of their holdings of government securities.

Anonymity was imperative because in this supply-and-demand market the primary security dealers were all competing with one another; for example, Salomon Brothers didn't want Merrill Lynch to know whether it was selling or buying, and how much. When it was important for an entity buying or selling government bonds to remain anonymous, they utilized the services of a firm like RMJ to act as an independent undisclosed broker, one of only four such middle-men companies.

Whenever RMJ acted as a broker to the primary security dealers, the amount we received as the broker was a fixed amount. This is a market in which tens of billion dollars of government securities trade each day. To broker these securities, we received $75 per million brokered; if we brokered $500 million in one trade conducted over a few seconds, our commission would be $37,500. Returns like this made RMJ a very profitable business.

While strong earnings with very little capital and only a few highly paid people were the pluses of the business, there were a number of minuses. The Wall Street primary security dealers universally felt that the brokers — or "deal pimps," as they often referred to them — were overcompensated for what they were doing. The dealers contended that the commissions received by us and in part passed through to the brokers were too high. Second, the success of our brokers was unofficially contingent upon their ability to have "quality" social contact with the individual dealers; in other words, the ability of RMJ brokers to personally entertain the primary dealers. They had to buddy up and spend a lot of money on their clients to get the business.

The broker routinely offered tickets to hockey and basketball games, limo rides, and front row seats at Broadway shows to satisfy their clients. This atmosphere bred some real Damon Runyan type characters. Our RMJ brokers went by nicknames like "The Rat," "The Mongoose," and "The Aardvark." The chasm between these young tyros with their large incomes and envelope-pushing entertainment and our more conservative bankers led to executive concern. It all challenged the sustainability and credibility of the non–capital-intensive earnings of RMJ which approached eight figures annually.

RMJ's brokers were typically in their late twenties and early thirties and inhabited a different world — a nocturnal blizzard of neon lights, nightclubs, limousines, wild parties, and God knows what. They were operating at breakneck speed, at burnout pace, spending enormous amounts and individually earning compensation of up to $1 million a year. Most of these guys used the "F" word as if it was an accepted industry substitute for every noun, verb, and adjective. I worked hard and with considerable caution about the circumstances under which we would bring them together with our high-profile bank executives. We kept somewhat quiet about RMJ; it was not a stop on the Security Pacific tour bus through New York City.

While the monthly $25,000 plus limousine bills caused us some concern, the RMJ boys were a perpetual source of fascination and apprehension as well as of earnings that were becoming meaningful to the bank. This was a side of finance I had not seen before; I was simultaneously repelled and enchanted.

We were aware that the Wall Street community wanted to clean up this market and to mitigate the potential for any public embarrassment for entertainment that went beyond tickets and limos to girls and drugs. Equally intent on preserving the dignity of the bank, we deciding to exit the business as their future came increasingly into question. We sold RMJ in 1986, after three years of operation, for $54 million, or $42 million more than it cost three years prior. Yet as a result we gave up the annual seven-figure earnings.

We had become convinced that selective companies, other brokers and similar activities operated in the U.S. and oversees could catapult us to the major leagues of the securities business. If we could be successful in our efforts, we would be positioned like only a few other world banks to seize an opportunity that had eluded U.S. banks since the passage of Glass–Steagall.

While many in our bank applauded these efforts, others hated the idea of exploring the opportunities of the securities business. And with reasons expressed by one of our "stay the course" senior executives who was opposed to our current direction: "I have a considerable aversion to any exorbitantly expensive endeavor whose ultimate success is based on companies that threaten our reputation as a family-based honorable bank or trying to read the minds of Congress."

Furthermore, he felt that analysts would soon find such a grandiose undertaking by a U.S. bank — let alone Security Pacific, a relative new-comer to the list of top five American banks — precipitous and confusing. "The concepts are alien, the ideas are embryonic, and the complexities enormous. The big payoff hinges on a dream."

When I first explained to this executive that I was moving forward on the purchase of fully capable securities firms in the United Kingdom, Canada, and Australia, I thought he would swallow his tongue.

"Good luck," he said in his soft, velvet voice, and added, "Are we going global, or buying trouble?"

The rest of the leadership team, however, was supportive. One of our team noted for a laugh, "I'm supportive of our efforts as we need earnings growth. But for God's sake, let's not step on our dicks in the process."

COLLABORATIVE – Business leaders should seek collaborative decisions even when significant elements of decisions are muted by the demanding expressions of stronger participants. Permitting thought and expression dominance to become coercive decision-making rather than a collaborative-based consensus process should be avoided.

The adventures into the securities business and the concluding results were somewhat mixed. The clearing and swaps businesses were both very successful but carried a marginally greater risk. The mutual fund business worked well, providing good overall value for the retail banking business. Other securities activities, all wrapped up in our Merchant Bank, were marginally successful, while a number of them did not realize their potential. The worldwide securities and brokerage companies, all part of the Merchant Bank, never reached expectations.

While we sounded and acted fearless in the expansion of our activities to advance into new markets and earnings opportunities ahead of our banking competition, we were all fearful to differing degrees. We really were acting with untested confidence that we could be successful at almost anything we wanted to try. In actuality, we did not have enough experience or knowledge to make these decisions without greater experience and study. As it turned out, fearless, quick draw decisions were not always successful and contributed to our overall failings.

> *FEARLESS – It is important for business leaders to remain fearless, yet cautious and careful when considering new markets and opportunities for growth.*

> *PROTECTIVE - Remaining protective and not undertaking risks that threaten the company's accomplishments and reputation are important to business leaders.*

GETTING CLOSER TO THE CUSTOMERS

Trying to find new markets, opportunities, and business interests is exciting but often creates a greater risk for the institution. It becomes very important to balance the expected earnings, growth, and risks in considering new or expanded opportunities. We were aggressively trying to grow non–interest, non–asset-based businesses to balance our extensive loan portfolio and commitment to real estate. What we discovered in the rapid expansion of our interest in securities-related functions was that it's significantly easier, with better opportunities for success, to expand the customer base or expand the level of business participation than to find or establish new markets. Instituting a strong customer focused sales culture through-out the organization is important to business growth success.

One of our growth strategies, employed during this early period, was attempting to become closer with our existing customers by offering new services or capturing more of their available business. In this process, we also wanted to locate and align ourselves with a greater number of pros-pects in order to gather new business as well as to expand existing busi-ness. Our key tactic was to implement strong business development tactics directed at select attractive markets that had strong margins.

As part of our Merchant Banking operations we had developed a unique business focused on offering repo and reverse-repo support to key Wall Street companies. It was a structurally complex business dependent on holding in custody and processing billions of dollars of U.S. government securities. The key to this business required holding the right to lend the securities held to any of the major Wall Street companies. The lent securi-ties would be secured by cash from the securities borrower, which would be invested overnight with the return split among the securities owner, the borrower, and us as the facilitator. This process was financially better than getting no return by just covering short positions with cash when the short could not be covered. Our margins for this non–asset intensive facilitation was exceptional.

We were aware that at that time Japanese financial institutions were the significant holders and long-term investors in U.S. government secu-rities. As with businesses of this type, we could grow the business and our profitability if we were to gather and hold in custody more government securities, knowing there was a substantial pipeline of demand for almost all these securities. This opportunity was available if the government secu-rities owners were willing to make more of these securities available for lending to the major Wall Street firms.

We met to discuss how we could attract more government securities for this use, knowing that direct sales and marketing in Japan were difficult.

"How can we gain greater support of the Japanese banks, insurance companies, and other financial institutions that are investing extensively in our government securities?" I asked.

The group manager responded with a very unique idea that made my head spin. "Our Japanese banking personal contacts are primarily with the third and fourth level executives in these banks. These are the individuals in control of the allocation and custody for their investments. We have, so far, been very successful in enhancing the yield on their government securities holdings by initiating this lending process. As a result, they are generally very happy, finding comfort in the backing of a major U.S. bank. I believe we could get more of their securities to lend if we could get personally closer to these executives. Obviously, we often have trouble in building a close and trusted relationship with them as a result of the different cultures and language." He paused and then continued. "My idea is to bring together our working executives, top company personnel, and one or two key recognized U.S. government officials for a weekend golfing extravaganza in Japan. I don't think this has ever been done before by any other U.S. company. They will eat this up and look to us and our bank with extreme respect and appreciation."

"Just think, these lower-tier Japanese executives are not yet of the stature to be Golf Club members. They all love golf and will generally do anything to have a weekend of business involving golf. Getting a weekend away from home and family for them is not a problem. I have worked with these bankers closely enough to know that this is a winner and will get us the results we want. There is the Kawana Resort with two courses that are available for such events. We would propose offering two days of golf, a great Japanese geisha-supported dinner, and a speech by a top U.S. government official. This would be a real prize and get us what we want: more government securities. I think it will cost us three or four hundred thousand dollars, but we'll get that back in a few weeks."

After a significant level of research to finalize the details, we had put the event together. Every Japanese banking official we invited attended, and we were able to invite the Head of the Federal Deposit Insurance Corporation as our government official to speak at the second night's dinner. We awarded sets of Ping irons to the better golfers, who interestingly happened to be our best customers.

Following the event, we assigned two of our best business development personnel to visit their Japanese counterparts. After two weeks of calls and comments, we had gathered enough new government securities in the repo and reverse/repo lending pool to pay for the golf tournament within the first month.

———————

Noting the success in Japan, six months later we employed a similar strategy entertaining our Wall Street based U.S. government securities dealers and Wall Street officials at a weekend event we arranged at Pebble Beach. This notorious resort and golf course became the weekend home to about ninety invited participants who were customers or prospects of our New York securities operations. This group was primarily the RMJ clientele.

The success of RMJ and the other brokers we operated depended on the securities dealers using our brokers and systems to buy and sell their large holdings of government securities and other forms of debt. While the dealers were extensively entertained in New York City, giving them a special moment to remember was our primary strategy for maintaining and growing these very profitable businesses. We had scheduled to play a Friday and Saturday round of golf on the famous Pebble Beach Golf Club and Spyglass Hill courses. A Friday dinner was followed on Saturday evening by a long cocktail hour, a special banquet dinner, and a speech offered by a key official of the New York Federal Reserve. Saturday evening closed with port and Courvoisier at the Pebble Beach bar.

In order to make this event special for the participants, we chartered a Boeing 737 to fly them directly to the Monterey Airport on Friday morning, returning Sunday evening. Competitive golf winners were awarded full Ping golf sets and bags at the Sunday brunch closing ceremony.

CREATIVE – Business leaders should be creative in finding new means by which customers and prospects can be favorably attracted and encouraged to do more business with the company.

DECISIVE – Business leaders should be willing to decisively make the differentiating decisions that can distinguish the company from its competitors.

CONFIDENT - Exhibiting confidence in the actions and anticipated outcome, even though controversial, is an important factor in leadership.

Such events not only left a memory with the participants but also allowed closer personal relationships with our top management attendees. In many respects, while the event was very expensive, it also left those who attended obligated to our securities operation and to place a strong level of business with New York based brokers.

Following the Pebble Beach trip, we were not disappointed in the results. During the first two weeks that the dealers returned to their Wall Street companies, we had sufficient business revenue to equal the prior year's two-week income plus pay all our costs of the golf event. The increased level of business continued for about a year. Overall, a very untraditional way for a bank to grow its business.

10

RESPONDING TO THE COMMUNITIES

SOUTH CENTRAL'S REDLINING CHALLENGE

Notwithstanding our aggressive growth and interest in the real estate development industry, we were also committed to other less exciting areas of the banking business. In this regard, we operated twenty-nine offices in what was described as South-Central Los Angeles and Watts serving mostly people of color, many of whom relied on some form of government assistance. These areas were primarily the home for African Americans and Hispanics with limited education and low-income jobs. It was identified by the predominance of youthful gangs, lack of public services, crime and a dearth of commercial involvement. In short, these were unattractive banking areas where many of the residents were struggling to survive. They had suffered from the Watts Riots in the 1960s and had become subject to marginal banking, commercial, and public service support. Among these offices, we were experiencing about a bank robbery each week along with identifying four or five of our employees each week who were taking cash from the bank or their customer accounts.

Because of poor real estate lending statistics in these areas, as reported by the Los Angeles Times, the banks and Security Pacific had been accused of "red-lining." This label meant that banks were unwilling to make real estate loans in defined areas. Generally, the real estate appraisal of a property was discounted because of the poorly maintained and unattractive physical and environmental condition of the area. In addition to this undervaluation, the loan advance was discounted again because of internal policies limiting a loan advance to no more than 40% to 50% of the appraised valuation, all for the same reasons. In addition, the borrower's income available to service the loan was reduced by discounting welfare and other government forms of income. As a result, the bank's avoidance of serving these communities was evident in the fact that the bank was meeting the requests of a little less than 10% of real estate loan applications coming from these areas.

We had been specifically called to task by the LA Times and various political figures in these areas. Under the gun, we were politely asked to discuss these issues by both Mark Ridley Thomas, a black city councilman, and the head of the Greenlining Coalition, an Oakland based public interest group. The meeting was scheduled for a Wednesday evening at a community center in the heart of Watts, a particularly decaying part of South Central Los Angeles. I decided to attend myself, given the public and even national discussions on this issue. I wanted to honestly know if we were doing the right thing under our lending policy or were we exercising a silent policy of redlining.

Given the ongoing unrest among the black community and the predominantly white-oriented business environment in Southern California, I was somewhat suspicious that we might not be doing the right thing. Preparing for the meeting, I was also concerned that a group of white officials from a major bank could be targets in an often-unsafe urban community. As a result, I took the community affairs vice president, the HRO, the Chief Credit Officer, and most importantly my personal security bodyguard. I had no idea what to expect or how public our meeting might be.

As relations between the community and the business interests, including banks were at a very low point, I wondered if we might be greeted with torches and pitchforks. The trip down to our meeting site was unsettling to all of us. I planned to introduce my bodyguard as another of our community relations officials so his participation wouldn't become an issue.

After mutual introductions, a cordial and very civil discussion began. I wanted to listen well and to know whether our actions were fair and appropriate to serve the community while maintaining a balanced risk in our home mortgage portfolio. They quickly noted that our loan approvals were, in their view, inappropriate compared to the obligations to the community resulting from our strong physical presence and the benefits derived from the deposit base of these offices.

We noted for the benefit of the city councilman that to generally improve area valuations it was also the city's responsibility to improve its services in terms of fire and policing protection within the higher risk areas, cleanliness, lighting on the streets, trash collection, medical services, and community counseling. We also noted that more pressure should be placed by all politicians on major developers, retailers, and food service providers to establish a greater commercial presence in the area. We didn't want to be the only business in their communities.

After considerable discussion of our current loan practices we collectively agreed that improving the community would require us to fairly value and advance against the properties. I noted that values should be based on comparable sales within the area but should not double discount the valuation as a result of the poor environment and area conditions, as had been the prior practice. These factors would have been included in the market comparable valuations. I also added that we should no longer discount government-sourced income or welfare, as it was often a more secure source of income than employment. We concluded that we should participate in improving the community by making a greater effort to jointly support these lower economic areas and their improvement in the months and years ahead. We noted, for the benefit of the councilman, that others, including the city officials and all city service functions, should also examine and reaffirm their commitments to these areas.

COLLABORATIVE – The ability to reach collaborative solutions to important problems that reconcile differences in the participants and meet a common goal is an essential quality of business leaders.

We had made progress and stayed safe personally, even though that latter way of thinking was perhaps a notion of the times. I commented to my bodyguard on the way back to our office that I could now more fully recognize the needs of these communities. After the discussion I had come to believe that most of the residents and community families not only wanted but also deserved what is essential to a fair good life: a safe, clean well-served community with the same opportunities available to those predominantly non-minority better served areas. I saw how wrong and unfair we had become in some of our attitudes and policies that had compromised our lending practices.

We made the changes in our policies, and in the months and years ahead the city also responded with a more coordinated, supportive service to the community. We also saw a growth in commercial services available in many of these areas. While I had been fearful, I knew that meeting the issues directly would help provide a better and broader community. When I later saw the difficulties arising from our troubled real estate loans and the growing losses, I thought back to this time and acknowledged what a speck in the sand this policy change had been to our company but how important it must have been to the community.

FINDING "THE MAN" IN THE COMMUNITY

With a predominance of branches in the South-Central Los Angeles and Watts community, the criminal nature of these areas required a considerable amount of management time. We were routinely experiencing robberies at most of our twenty-nine local community offices. Since we had accepted the cost of stolen property and cash as a result of these events, our primary effort was to ensure the safety of our employees and customers. It was a statistical fact that a few of these offices had become a high priority for the crooks. Freeway access and branches without guards were both high criteria targets for the intended robbers.

One such branch, located at Manchester and Vermont, was experiencing unusually heavy robbery activity. We assigned a guard to the branch, but this didn't quell the interest in the bank as a high-priority robbery target. We were experiencing a robbery during business hours nearly every other week.

Our employees were in a state of near panic, since most occurrences included armed participants. In addition to robberies, at least once a month an employee's car battery or tires was stolen from the parking lot during the work day. Our practice was to employ un-armed guards to avoid any personal harm, most often using them to patrol and walk the employees to their cars after hours.

We were having serious trouble in keeping employees as these issues got out of hand. This troubled branch situation had moved to the water cooler conversation at many of our offices with increasing employee stress. We were seriously struggled to get replacements for a growing employee exit from many of the area branches. Our complaints to the Los Angeles police and the FBI offered little help in our effort. I realized that without a workable solution in the next few weeks we would struggle to keep some of these branches open. Without law enforcement assistance, I focused my attention on finding someone outside of the local government or police, who was a major part of the community, and could help us find a solution.

I asked the branch manager, "Who is 'the man' who can make things happen when the government fails to respond?"

"You have to see Ted Watkins," he said. "I will introduce you. He is 'the man.' Everyone loves and respects him. He works to create jobs, even trains bank tellers for employment."

Two weeks later I met Ted at the branch and we left for some unknown location in his gold Lincoln Continental convertible with leopard skin seat covers. I sat down and noticed a gun lying on the seat between us. Not taking my eye off the pistol, I asked him to show me his teller training facility.

After telling me that I was lucky to be with him or I wouldn't be safe in this area, he began to explain his training operation. "We get state support to train these young people to work in a bank. We take on about forty at a time to train them over a six-month period. We begin by teaching them how to get up on time, how to catch a bus, and how to dress for work. Then, we get into handling banking transactions."

"I can't believe that," I noted, "because we try to train them in about two weeks to become a qualified teller. I guess that our young people have a more traditional background and understanding of bank accounts," I responded. "But Ted, what I wanted to talk to you about is the weekly robberies and trouble we are experiencing at our branch. I have to find a way to make the robberies and parking lot instances stop or frankly I will have no choice but to close the office. I wondered if you can help me"

"Okay, but first let's take a look at my facility," he said.

We arrived at a somewhat older, rundown industrial warehouse, walked in, and saw a lot of old vintage teller equipment and perhaps ten trainers and about forty students.

"We graduate about 40% of our students since a lot of the young people can't or prove to be unwilling to make the commitment to six months training at a minimum wage," he noted.

The teller training was rather standard and detailed in the depth of coverage. It was very consistent with our style and methods. I knew we could use these people in our operation, especially if they continued to leave our branches, but had never heard of Ted's teller training operation until this moment.

We sat down, and I began to talk. "Look Ted, I want to make a deal with you. If you can stop our robberies, I will get you all new equipment for your training facility and hire all your graduates. Can you do it?

"I think that can happen," he said. "Don't do anything until the robberies stop, but I know they will."

That branch didn't have a robbery for the next three years, and we got a continuing number of trained tellers for our operations.

"The Man" had spoken loudly.

FEARLESS – The ability to act without fear or concern that the resolution of difficult situations may not work or be out of line with traditional practices is an important element of strong business leaders.

SERVING AS PART OF THE STATE MESS

About three years prior to our tumultuous credit problems, I was invited by the California Governor Pete Wilson, a republican, to become the banking-related designee to the State Teachers Retirement System or STRS, as it was more commonly known. At the time I questioned how spending a day a month in Sacramento would enhance my career or help Security Pacific advance its business interests.

My concerns about the time commitment was magnified during my first STRS board meeting about a week later. At that time, STRS had a pension fund of bit over $8 billion under its oversight, control, and part of its fiduciary responsibility. Sharing this responsibility on the board with me was a designated insurance industry designee, both the California State Treasurer and Controller (neither of whom attended the meetings except through a designee), a state legislator, and three members of the State Teachers Union.

The largest issue and concern that arose from the first meeting was a legally mandated but overlooked change in regulations that required STRS to structure a relationship with independent outside investment managers. These new managers were required to be contractually employed within the next thirty days; otherwise the funds would become unmanaged, threatening the trustee's fulfillment of their fiduciary responsibility. This seemed a nearly impossible task without an extensive time commitment on the part of the board trustees. It would be necessary to conduct an extended selection process to define and contract with qualified investment managers.

To complicate this issue, I became quickly aware that decision-making on this new board was difficult, due to the political interest of the board participants and my quick recognition that the board's chairperson was an alcoholic who was not under any form of treatment. She was fully disorganized and not able to communicate with any clarity or bring issues and votes to any conclusion. She was often incoherent and stumbling, however able to extend the meetings for hours at a time with very little action, discussion, or understanding.

Each meeting during this period was painfully long, resulting in this new challenge occupying nearly 50% of my available work hours as travel to and from Sacrament was extensive. I was convinced, however that without a full commitment to the issues, we could all be challenged for not meeting our fiduciary responsibilities.

My concern was whether I would be protected as an employee of the bank against any lawsuit launched against both me, the bank, or STRS for failure to meet the board responsibility. I had become quickly aware that this board was totally dysfunctional and was failing to meet its fiduciary duties. As with most similar issues, the legal departments of both the bank and STRS wanted more time and information to give me assurance of my protection.

PATIENT – Remaining patient in working through difficulties or periods that are outside expectations or personal experiences is an important quality of business leaders.

While I was learning from the experience, I quickly became aware that political minds are not business minds. While we were expected to make logical structured business-related decisions, the political thinking process was driven by power, influence, and anything at the opposite end of the spectrum of good business logic and thinking.

Working twelve to eighteen hours a day for over two straight weeks and at times becoming personally obstinate with all the obstacles, the trustee group finally successfully hired investment managers within the thirty-day time frame I learned to quickly despise my new role on the board and to dislike the political process, politicians, and related political bureaucrats. If community service was the issue, I would rather have worked in a local soup kitchen.

COMMUNICATIVE – It is important for business leaders to demonstrate understanding and tolerance in communicating with those with whom there is disagreement, but to stand firm in the effort to fulfill the known objectives.

I became very cynical and negative toward the continuing process of monthly meetings because I had developed a bad, distorted, and selfish attitude toward most all politicians and government workers. I concluded that my service served no purpose in my career nor was participating a positive for its political and regulatory impact on Security Pacific.

I quickly realized that the responsibility was talking too much time and energy and that my negative attitude was not constructive to either STRS or the bank. I wanted to resign but realized that following through with my mental threat would cause an embarrassment for Security Pacific among the state political body. It became clear that it would be necessary that I find another escape.

My solution was to follow the guidance of the State's Comptroller and Treasurer and look for a designee to serve as my representative. I was surprised, but this was acceptable legally and to the other members of the board. Perhaps my bad attitude added to the board's willingness to accept this action. It all concluded well, and I was never sued over the three years I served on the board. In the end, the board chairperson never showed up sober, the politicians continued to want their backs patted, and the governor sent me a nice wall plaque for my service, probably having no idea who I was or had accomplished.

11

SEEKING A CHANGED ENVIRONMENT

BEGGING THE REGULATORS FOR HELP

In the period leading up to our difficulties in 1990 I was appointed to serve on the board of the American Bankers Association, the spokesperson of most American banks. As part of the ABA, I participated in several animated discussions about the new regulatory environment and the implementation of regulations associated with FIRREA. Strong feelings about this new legislation, enacted to prevent a recurrence of the savings and loan collapse, had been stirred up in opposition to FIRREA's revised real estate valuation provisions. The loudest voices came from banks that held large and concentrated real estate portfolios. As the talks continued we knew that if we were to find any relief, it would be necessary for the board to address its concerns directly to the top regulators.

Two months later, in October 1990, we convened an emergency meeting of the ABA board in Orlando, Florida during the annual member's meeting. We requested and received a private meeting of the board with Bill Seidman, the head of the Federal Deposit Insurance Corporation, Bob Clarke, the Comptroller of the Currency, and Alan Greenspan, Chairman of the Federal Reserve Board.

For whatever reason, perhaps because I appeared to feel exceedingly passionate about these issues — and for good reason — I was selected to be the spokesperson to vocalize the ABA's concerns with FIRREA.

I was unaware of the strength or weakness of my personal relationship with the regulatory bodies but knew that our bank had historically been openly critical of them. Most recently, I was sure they would have growing concerns about our slumping real estate portfolio. As a result, I was unsure if I was the best spokesperson on this issue and how much sway I held with them. I was also concerned that I'd intensified their antipathy toward Security Pacific by delivering speeches in which I made comments like:

"Our government response to recent savings and loan problems has been overly aggressive in defanging the banks, leaving them on a diet of soft food and pablum. Their first so-called corrective measure was the Financial Institutions Recovery and Reform Act of 1989, commonly called FIRREA. Because much of the savings and loan problem was the result of aggressive real estate lending, this law, as promulgated, requires the exclusive use of outside appraisals to support real estate loans. That sounds like a very logical move. But the law also mandates that the appraisals be on an "as is now" basis. In other words, what a single buyer would pay for an entire project within a twelve-month period. This in effect required that real estate be marked to the current market price. This is a new concept in banking that ignored the historical valuation process, which looked at periodic economic downturns as only a temporary impairment to the property's value. The regulators seemed to ignore the fact that if the banks had been aware of such a drastic change, they would never have made many of the loans in the first place. This is closing the barn door after the horse has left the stable and is totally unfair."

In short, discrediting FIRREA had become my obsession, my crusade, my raison d'être, but any impact I might have was very questionable.

UNDERSTAND PRACTICES AND STANDARDS – Business leaders should have a current awareness and knowledge of regulations and industry practices that are essential to effectively managing the company.

Approximately forty members of the ABA board attended the session, which was held in the auxiliary conference room of the ABA headquarters hotel in Orlando.

The tone of the meeting was very civilized. Federal Reserve chair Alan Greenspan and the other regulators all looked attentive and interested in what we had to say. After introductions and salutations, I was permitted to lay the foundation of the ABA's case.

"I will be as concise as possible. Our concern is with the new emerging regulatory environment and particularly the appraisal valuation provisions set forth in FIRREA. In the past decade, hand in hand with the assistance of the government, banks have weathered a triad of considerable crises. I speak specifically, of course, of the agricultural crisis, the Leveraged Buyout matters, and the crisis in the developing countries. Now we face a fourth: the simultaneous deterioration of worldwide economies and the toll this is expected to take on the real estate industry, especially the portfolios of many large banks that specialize in real estate lending. The application of FIRREA, its passage into law, and the subsequent impact of its provisions — specifically Subsection C, Appraisal — was not something that we foresaw, and its ramifications are significant and, in many cases, expected to be severe.

"The government, and we applaud them for it, had not, however, dealt so drastically with our prior crises. Instead they worked closely with the industry and many specific banks, and in each case these problems resolved themselves over time.

"More recently, when weather anomalies adversely affected the value of farm loans and seriously impaired the agricultural market, the government successfully converted what appeared to be an imminent crisis into a long-term solution. Had those who drafted FIRREA taken the same approach to the agricultural crisis, small banks all over the Midwest would have had to write off all their loans and these circumstances would have destroyed perhaps five thousand banks. But government handled it with care and foresight: you allowed the banks to ride it out, recalibrate the loans on a long-term basis, and the values ultimately rekindled as the economy rebounded.

In the mid-1980s, when the less developed countries were unable to repay huge sums of debt, government, with foresight and care, converted what appeared to be an imminent crisis into a long-term solution. Had analogous valuation restrictions been imposed on banks during the Lesser Developed Country credit crisis, we would have witnessed the failure of most of the top ten banks in this country.

"It seems to us that government today should be just as interested in the survival of the banks, as the engines of our economy, as they were during other difficult times in the 1980s.

"The thesis I am setting forth is that, unlike in prior crises, the regulators seem to be, for want of a better expression, off on a destructive rather than a constructive mission, and they are causing the annihilation of our ability to continue to advance credit to many sectors of our economy such as real estate and others that banks have traditionally supported. Banks are having to pull in their reins in terms of their lending standards and policies to all market segments because of the new fear engendered by regulators in their aggressive examination of portfolios under the new FIRREA-based regulations.

"I ask you to consider the ramifications of this provision to the economy.

"While we are aware of the theory behind FIRREA's stipulation that real estate and assets be valued for collateral purposes on a twelve-month liquidation basis, if regulators rigidly maintain this as a precept for examination it will basically destroy the real estate industry and lubricate the further deterioration of the U.S. economy. And I don't believe this to be an overstatement. FIRREA casts a dark shadow over all the banks in the United States. While we understand that its purpose is to facilitate the clean-up of the savings and loan debacle, its unintended effect will be to cripple banks across this country for many years!

"Because lending is the engine of economic growth, it logically follows that once this engine shuts off, the economy will slow more and more. Fewer customers will be able to obtain a loan; no longer will our customers be able to readily purchase machinery, build a business, or develop property. Jobs will be lost, and the middle market will be the hardest hit.

ORGANIZED – Organizing discussions in a clear, concise, and understandable way is important to effective leadership when attempting to gain the reconsideration of critical issues.

"While we fully recognize that we are in weakened economic times, it is suggested that we be permitted to deal with the current crisis the way we dealt with the Lesser Developed Country crisis and that you allow us to pursue a long-term solution to a severe problem rather than impose short-term solutions. We propose that you allow us to carry real estate loans at a value that anticipates a return to a stronger economy and the value-enhancement that development of a property provides. This approach will be a change to a valuation process that currently results in reducing bank capital and could have a very deep bottom. We believe it is premature, drastic, and draconian to write these properties and loans down as is now being prescribed. Thank you for your time and attention."

I sat down.

Alan Greenspan didn't take long to compose his response. "We certainly understand what you are saying, and we are sympathetic to your view. And we are aware that this is a very serious difficulty with formidable ramifications. However, the fact remains FIRREA is a mandate of Congress and it is our job to enforce it."

"Do you believe that Congress fully comprehends the inevitable and anticipated consequences of that provision, and its detrimental effect not only on banks but on the ability of banks to continue lending?" I asked.

Greenspan replied, "That I can't say with absolute certainty. One would hope that Congress would extrapolate the potential consequence of any legislation as far-reaching as that set forth in FIRREA. What I can say with a measure of certainty is that FIRREA was passed into law, and that it cannot be unpassed. FIRREA is a congressional expression of dismay and impatience with the costly financial events of the past decade."

"Regardless of the harm it may cause to banks?"

"Regardless or despite the harm it may cause. And FIRREA, they feel, is the way to handle it."

As Greenspan replied, I could see every ABA eye in the room glaze over, not in boredom but anguish.

"Mr. Clarke," I asked the comptroller of the currency, "do you think it is possible for the regulators to exercise some latitude about the rigidity with which they demand banks enact that provision? May they be empowered to use their own good judgment?" What I was asking was, could regulators be made to use the gift of common sense that God gave them when deciding whether a bank should write down real estate loans whose outlook is strong, notwithstanding a harsh appraisal?

The answer was: "We feel the regulators were rebuked with a rather firm hand for what happened to the savings and loan industry, and it is our job to make sure it never happens again and to see that the mandate of Congress is executed. This is what Congress does, this is what Congress wants, and it is our job to enforce the will of Congress."

"Very well. And you realize the impact this will have on banks?"

"We, as a government, are going to have to accept whatever fallout is the side effect of this act."

"So, you're saying, if I hear you correctly, this is the way it's going to be, and you guys had better get used to it."

DISCIPLINED - Business leaders should be disciplined in listening well and responding clearly to sensitive situations

COMMUNICATIVE - Listening well and considering the views of others in order to communicate a constructive response is important for business leaders.

"I'm afraid that's about the size of it."

When the forty directors of the ABA filed out of that conference room, we were dazed. There would be no recourse, no escape hatch. We were stuck.

I walked away shaking my head. Banks had a very serious problem and Security Pacific, in particular, was facing a chasm. Things had changed, and government was not going to help us this time. Congress saw banks as the enemy. And regulators, I feared, would no longer be mere annoyances but would become avenging angels. We were no longer "too big to fail."

THE CALIFORNIA GOVERNOR WON'T LISTEN

In the environment of growing credit issues, I was haunted by the belief that the California economy might be falling into the Pacific Ocean. I also knew that if the state, local, or national government stepped forward with any more legislative "quick fixes" that were lethal injections in disguise, our problems would increase with little hope of improving. For these reasons, I could see that the market gyrations were most likely a precursor to a broader economic disaster. As a result, I continued to seek the recognition and assistance of anyone capable of stabilizing California. Strangely, I wasn't sure our politicians understood what was happening. And I wasn't alone.

I was a member of the California Business Roundtable, an association of the one hundred largest companies in the state. We met routinely to discuss the kaleidoscope of issues that faced California and its business community. As fate would have it, I was the chairperson of the public policy subcommittee, which dealt directly with state government policy.

The Roundtable arrived at a consensus: we had to face Governor Pete Wilson head on. Wilson's staff had predicted 3% job growth for 1991. Who was he kidding? We wondered why he had his head in the sand. We universally felt that California's economy was a falling comet waiting to crash into the state. Each month more businesses were departing California to find more economic and tax friendly environments, and it seemed that the state leaders wouldn't admit the problem, let alone do anything about it.

How could the governor lead this state or even decide what was best for California business if he didn't understand or, worse, ignored the realistic, front-line economic outlook of the very people in the best position to know?

As chairman of the subcommittee, I was chosen to lead a group to meet with Governor Wilson and his staff along with other members of the committee. Our goal was to encourage the governor to implore businesses to remain in California and to actively solicit new business to move to the state. We would urge Wilson to mount a counteroffensive against governors from the south and states as nearby as Oregon and Utah that sought to entice business away from California and its anemic economy.

We arrived at this crucial meeting prepared. Our attitude was upbeat, our agenda ambitious, and our case solid. We felt our recommendations were logical, achievable, and in everyone's best interest.

ORGANIZED – Business leaders should structure elements of open issues in an organized, constructive, and consistent manner.

Wilson entered. Before the first word had been spoken, he seemed impatient to leave. He sat on the corner of his chair, his knee gyrating, one foot pointed at the door and his eye fixed on the wall clock behind me. "Morning, gentlemen."

Governor Wilson is not like a Charles Keating or Donald Trump. He could slump past you on a street corner without you ever knowing you'd been in the proximity of leadership. His posture was feeble, and no one will ever accuse Wilson of speaking with great conviction.

But what we had going for us, we thought, was common sense and in the greater interest of California.

We introduced ourselves. Governor Wilson, a Republican, was familiar with the Business Roundtable, but our presence did not appear to interest him. Perhaps we had caught him at an inopportune time. Animated by his impatience, I rapidly explained our concerns and proposed our solutions, which primarily involved a joint business and government strategy to keep businesses and jobs in California. I explained that as part of this strategy each of our companies would commit to not move operations out of the state, and hopefully, he would embark on a specific effort to jawbone any other company contemplating a move out of the state. No money, no tax relief, just a joint effort to keep jobs in the state and to hopefully stabilize the economy. Wilson squinted at me as if through a dense fog.

When I alluded to his participation in our plan, he abruptly interrupted me. His cheeks puffed out and his face went red as he addressed us in a peremptory tone. "You don't even need to tell me about all this. I am very aware of all that," he said in a condescending rasp. "What you probably don't realize is that the real culprit here is not the governor's office, it's not even the economy. You know who it is? It's Willie Brown," he revealed. Mr. Brown was the Speaker of the Assembly, an entrenched and powerful African-American Democratic legislator with a vociferous share of supporters and detractors. "Willie Brown, with his distinctly strong liberal bias, is at constant odds with me."

For the next fifteen minutes, it was Willie Brown this and Willie Brown that. "It's all Willie Brown's fault," Wilson continued. "He holds the key to all our problems in the palm of his hand and he will not let go." To believe Wilson's lament, all that had ever gone wrong in the state of California was directly traceable to the nefarious designs of Willie Brown.

Governor Wilson's tirade handily filled the time he'd allotted for our meeting. Rather than discuss the impact of a wan economy on state business, we watched as Governor Wilson raised his voice, cleared his throat, hemmed and hawed, screwed up his face, and damned everything there was too damn about Willie Brown. "He's the villain in this sad charade. Now if you'll excuse me."

"Governor, one more moment of your time, if I may." Innocently believing there was no problem that could not be solved by reasonable people who put their minds to it, I foolishly suggested we include Willie Brown in our discussions. "If Mr. Brown is the obstacle, let's sit down with him and calmly hash out these problems. Certainly, we can also agree on some reasonable steps. Liberal or Conservative, it's in no one's best interest, not even Willie Brown's, for the state economy to collapse."

"You don't know Willie Brown." Again, Wilson shot for the exit.

"Governor, why on earth would anyone stand in the way of a plan whose purpose is to keep jobs in California? Certainly, there could be other partial solutions such as trim redundancy, streamline government, a stimulus package?"

"You don't understand," Wilson bellowed. "You have no idea who Willie Brown is or what he's capable of. That man is impossible. There's no talking to him. There's nothing you can do, nothing I can do, nothing anybody can do about Willie Brown." Again, the door. "It was a real pleasure speaking with you gentlemen."

Wilson spun around like a wind-up toy when I made a final appeal. "Governor, forgetting about Willie Brown for one second, we think you should make a visible effort to get behind the business community. Would you consider personal involvement in our plan to keep jobs in California, or perhaps establish a staff operation whose aim would be to work with companies contemplating a move as well as working to attract new employers to the state?"

Wilson shook his head. "The economy, according to my staff, is certainly on the mend, and we have that to look forward to. And I've got too many other initiatives to fight right now."

We thanked him, and he pushed us out of the room as quickly as he could without appearing rude.

COLLATERATIVE – It is preferable that business leaders seek solutions that resolve issues with collaborative thinking.

My colleagues and I briefly lamented the time and effort we'd put into our presentation. I felt we had wasted our time and the governor had abdicated his job and responsibility to Willie Brown.

SHUTTERING THE PERKS

When serious trouble with the possibility of company failure is possible, the CEO is generally willing to do almost anything to improve the situation. In these situations, the boss can be expected to move to emergency management mode. This means that decisions will be made that have the greatest impact on saving or improving the viability of the institution. Our bank was in serious trouble, and I was aware that among other actions we had to save every penny we could in our effort to survive. To begin this process, we explored all options for savings, economies, and efficiencies that could make a significant contribution to our continued existence.

This examination included reviewing the activities we wanted and enjoyed in our business but didn't really need. I realized that some forms of spending and the perception thereof are important both from the cost savings as well as the public view of the company's leadership. With this in mind, my staff conducted an examination of how and why we spent every cent of our money, and the savings that could be realized.

Among all the matters considered, travel and entertainment are generally at the top of the list of any examination. The class, place, and style of travel and overnight hotels were, for us, a matter of policy and were set by title, purpose, and length of trip. More significant in the consideration was the need and use of our three private jets, including a Gulfstream III, a helicopter, plus a pleasure boat in Hong Kong, two condos in New York, and a home in Sun Valley. Most of these amenities were to make life easier and faster for our senior officers. The rationale for the bigger costly aircraft was to allow us to conveniently visit customers, offices, and events we would otherwise not find easily accessible or a priority of our use of time.

During good times, such conveniences are justifiable, but in troubled times, these items are generally the first to be eliminated in the effort to lower overall costs. After discussing our options, we felt it would be better to sell all of the aircraft and the private hanger, dismiss the staff, and sublease the New York condos. We also no longer found any reason or justification for keeping the boat or Sun Valley home. Not only would the savings help our cash flow, these items all had public visibility and taking the steps to unload them added to the credibility of management.

As part of the staff examination, we agreed that we would declare a hiring freeze and temporarily eliminate performance bonus payments, except for sales commissions, for a majority of our employees. This was to become policy until matters improved. Along with these steps, we began extending a retention program for employees in critical or customer controlling positions; we also initiated an early retirement program for many positions that were no longer critical to our existence.

DECISIVE – Business leaders should be clear and decisive when addressing matters that may be significantly unpopular but helpful to the company.

Both the press and the regulators had extensive interest in what we were considering in these areas and routinely asked the questions as a test of our management qualities and concern for the problems. During a visit from the Los Angeles Times, the reporter spent considerable time viewing the many decorative items and paintings in our executive office space and particularly in my office before beginning an interview.

His first question was, "Where did you get all of the paintings by California artists and do you collect the pieces of art and paintings I've noted in your office? Are you an art collector?"

Realizing this was a set-up question to establish me as someone other than an officer concerned about the bank, I responded, "First, I am not an art collector and really don't pay any attention to these pieces. They were all part of the interior decoration of the floor before I was at this level. My concern is the investor shareholders, employees, customers, and our communities. I work and think about what helps each of them." In other words, up yours. Later and in response to his comments, I did have the larger art pieces and the office items removed and placed into storage.

To add credibility to these steps I felt it was advisable to inform the board of directors of the intended changes. When I did, it became apparent that some were still somewhat ignorant as to the depth of the problems. When informed, several wondered out loud if this was all necessary. One of the directors somewhat naively commented. "Does this mean that the helicopter won't be available to bring me to the board and audit committee meeting each month?"

My answer was very straightforward. "Our air force is going out of business now, and I would suggest that if you feel this transportation is essential, you can certainly charter your own alternate travel means, but you will have to personally bear the cost."

12

BAILING OUT

COZYING UP TO A RICH UNCLE

In mid-summer of 1991 following the late 1990 special charges, the collapse of the Wells Fargo merger, and the funding crisis, I received a personal call from Dick Rosenberg, the Bank of America CEO, suggested we once again explore a possible merger between our two banks. Later that week, I flew to San Francisco to meet with Dick in a private room at the Ritz Carlton Hotel. We met that day in strict secrecy to continue our early Spring discussions. To disguise our meeting, I told my office that I was meeting, once again, with the Federal Reserve.

In the Spring, I had responded to his earlier call to meet and discuss a merger, recognizing that a continuing economic decline could spell doom for Security Pacific. After examining our weakened financial position, events of the prior months, and a continuing uncertain economic outlook, I had concluded that the best solution for the investor shareholders and everyone with an interest in our bank, was to find a rich uncle who was willing to add meaningful capital support to our declining loans. A merger, even if lopsided, would do that, and I felt that it was considerably more attractive than trying to raise new capital for a weakened company with a depressed stock price. The only costs of such a merger, I recognized, would be shattering our history and relinquishing most of our collective power and control.

We met several times that Spring but had concluded that the issues and uncertainty with our bank were too great to discuss in any detail the idea of combining our banks. I had, since those Spring discussions, worked hard, and had been successful in resolving and closing many unresolved matters related to the bank, most specifically the shuttering of the Merchant Bank. I wanted to make Security Pacific look as clean and understandable as possible, remembering the glitches evident in the effort to merge with Wells. I had dressed up the doll, even though it was on life-support. This meeting would be just he and I—no facilitators, no attorneys, not even an assistant to take notes.

Dick Rosenberg had joined Bank of America in the mid-1980s, after a short stint at Crocker Bank following his work and numerous run-ins with Carl Reichardt at Wells Fargo. He had joined Bank of America following a period of unbridled early 1980s decline, resulting in the bank board's aggressive interest in his services in order to create a quick turnaround. Initially, he was the executive in charge of the branches at Bank of America's Seafirst operation in Seattle, Washington, but he was called to its San Francisco headquarters in 1987. In late 1989, Rosenberg took over the top job as its Chief Executive Officer. He was nearly as new on the job as me. This was our first face to face meeting in this new round of discussions. Initially I found him to be warm and friendly; but as our talk progressed, he seemed to be pre-programed or rehearsed for this initial discussion..

The first thing Rosenberg insisted, as our meeting began, was to jointly sign a confidentiality agreement. He wanted to stimulate the free flow of classified financial data between our two organizations and, most important for him—for reasons that would become crystal clear in a matter of days— stipulate that during our discussions we would be prohibited from conducting any merger discussions with another bank. The exclusivity clause forbade either one of us from talking directly or indirectly with others about anything to do with our meetings. He wanted no leaks about what we were doing.

After bringing him up to date on our condition and the steps we had taken to close the uncertainties that were a concern at our Spring meeting we quickly got into the details of a possible combination of our two companies.

His single-minded fervor was a real godsend. I speculated that the thing driving this man was his uncertainty about the interest Wells Fargo might have in Security Pacific. His worst nightmare realized would be for Wells Fargo to learn of our meeting and try to intervene with a competitive merger deal. Much of this was driven by his dislike for the way he was treated by Carl Reichardt, the head of Wells Fargo, who had purportedly fired Rosenberg twice: once from the Wells Fargo executive team and the second time a few months later when Wells bought Crocker National Bank after Rosenberg joined their executive team.

During the eleven days of negotiation to follow and extending through the next nine months of the process Rosenberg never uttered the Wells Fargo CEO's name. Not once, not ever, not even in casual passing; he didn't even want me to think about Wells Fargo. He didn't want me to joke about Wells Fargo. And I didn't want to invoke the name for fear that he might ask me point-blank if they posed a threat to the deal. I would have to confess that as far as I knew Wells had no further interest whatsoever in reviving discussions or better said in merging with Security Pacific. A technically true statement.

By divulging my previous experience and the ultimate Wells' disinterest, I would have lost an important component and point of leverage that was very important to my negotiating power.

Only a few weeks earlier, Reuters News Service had unwittingly aggravated Rosenberg's fear of Wells Fargo by regurgitating the rumor of a Security Pacific–Wells Fargo merger and reporting that such a merger was "attractive and compelling to both shareholders."

This first of the revived meetings went well in rekindling the initial discussions we'd had in the Spring. We reiterated our belief in the strategic significance and benefits to both parties, the understanding relative to keeping the Bank of America name, and that he would be the ongoing CEO. If the merger could be completed, it would be significant that the combined banks would be the largest bank headquartered in the United States. We briefly discussed the exchange ratio but demurred on setting it firmly until we'd exchanged data, done additional analysis, and consulted with staff and our respective investment bankers. We agreed to meet again later that week to discuss our findings, specify the exchange ratio, and explore the social issues of such a large merger.

Over the several days following our initial summer meeting we exchanged information like two men playing Beat the Clock in what amounted to an accelerated due diligence. A very small circle of executives at both companies knew about the discussions.

His people commenced an examination of our loan portfolio; mine of his. We quizzed each other to understand many of the specifics of our individual operations. Our financial and credit people, along with our investment bankers, burned the wick at both ends to comprehend the financial health of the respective institutions. Their ancillary diligence freed us to collectively consider the exchange ratio and the expected social issues: the ongoing management team, who's in and who's out, location of headquarters, board membership, savings benefits, and the reality of layoffs, including displacement, compensation, and the impact job cuts would have on our customers and communities.

Because we had both done abundant "homework" on the deal already, these were not cold and calculating marathon debates. The mood was brisk and cordial and our moons seemed to be aligned. We discussed issues openly and frankly without any unusual differences. Rosenberg was a good negotiator who communicated clearly and listened well. But I knew I needed his company and its capital to offset our loan difficulties, regulatory pressure, and investor as well as employee concerns. Most importantly I knew I must find a way to survive continuing economic and loan portfolio weaknesses.

But he also wanted absolute understanding and control. He could not abide the presence of one loose shoestring or a single department or subsidiary whose complexity eluded his understanding. The depth of his knowledge was unquestionable in many areas, but shallow, as if by design, in others. He appeared to have limited curiosity about our most unusual and often lucrative subsidiaries. He did not question our swaps and derivatives portfolio, which had unnerved Reichardt and Wells. All this I found ominous.

FINANCIAL UNDERSTANDING – In complex financial transactions, management should understand the financial implications of the intended arrangement. This includes an understanding of accounting, tax, investment, and financial elements as well as other matters associated with combining financial structures. The ability of business leaders to think, understand, and quickly adjust to changing financial structures or arrangements is important.

We met again that Friday. Our discussions were positive, at times euphoric. He wanted to keep the new Bank of America's monolithic headquarters in San Francisco at its present location but agreed to retain Security Pacific's downtown office space in Los Angeles as the new Bank of America's southern California headquarters.

In our first encounter, he had expressed some reluctance at the notion of equal boards, but he now relented: "I know a true merger has equal boards, and I think we should structure our new company that way."

We agreed. The new board of directors would consist of fifteen Bank of America directors and fifteen from Security Pacific. The name of the surviving entity would be Bank of America, and it would be known throughout the consolidation process as the New Bank of America.

Dick and I enumerated a joint-staff approval policy for key management, stating that beyond the selection of the eight or nine senior executives any other nominees would require the signatures and approval of both of us. This was important in formulating an equitable personnel program: in every position we would choose the candidate most qualified for the job based on skill level, experience, and track record, the best and the brightest: the best auditor, the best attorney, the best Chief Credit Officer, and so forth.

Finally, he offered — and I agreed — that following his retirement in about four years at age sixty-five and contingent upon board approval I would replace him as chief executive officer. This would be a specific stipulation of any agreement we finalized. While not a game-breaker for me, I accepted this fact. But down deep I was not sure I wanted to succeed Rosenberg and run the New Bank of America or in the end that the regulators would allow that to happen.

This experience was a classic example of compromising and collaborating in an effort to reach an agreement. While each party had a separate priority and sense of urgency, in reaching agreement there was a clear meeting of the minds and concessions made by both of us.

COLLABEORATIVE – *Listening and reasoning with all participants to achieve the fairest collaborative understanding is important to business leaders.*

Then, we got down to brass tacks: the exchange ratio. I had reviewed the analysis and had decided on what I thought was a fair exchange ratio. He and I compared respective analyses and considered what this consolidation would mean in a broad sense for both investor shareholder groups. After considerable discussion we arrived at an exchange ratio based on the market value capitalization of each company over the prior thirty days, and one that gave respective investor shareholders an equal part of the benefits of the combined efficiencies we expected to realize.

The meeting ended on this high note, with our agreement to attempt to finalize our understanding by the conclusion of the following week.

With our agreement on the exchange rate, we turned the calculations over to our investment bankers to let them fine-tune the numbers. Bank of America hired Morgan Stanley; we brought in First Boston. They collectively studied the exchange ratio with representatives from Morgan Stanley.

The next week the First Boston people strode into my office in a mischievous mood. "We've completed our analysis and they've completed theirs. We believe, after discussing the numbers with Morgan Stanley, that we can obtain a better exchange ratio."

"Better than we already have?" I asked wonderingly. "Why would they?"

"In a word: terror. Morgan Stanley's people feel that Wells Fargo poses a lingering threat to the potential deal. They believe you have had some discussions with Wells and are familiar with the numbers of both potential partners. They feel that Wells could step in after a deal is announced with a preemptory bid, a higher offer that might be better for the Security Pacific investor shareholders." What they don't know is that these discussions had already ended without any open opportunity to continue the talks.

"But the exchange ratio is good," I said. "It's fair to both sides. This is supposed to be a merger, not an auction." I was grateful for the deal we'd arranged; the last thing on my mind was putting the squeeze on Dick, and I told him as much. "I'd rather not disturb the equation we already have and risk jeopardizing the deal or the specific terms. I mean, I almost don't want to breathe on the exchange ratio. You know that I am not dealing from any particular strength other than their fear of Wells."

"Understood, Bob. I just want you to be aware, and as your investment bankers we would be delinquent not to say so: we think the money is there."

He smiled, shrugged, and walked toward the door.

"Hold on, Come back."

I continued. "Really, I'm quite satisfied with what we've arranged. And it's my job to make this deal happen. But, having said that, I'm not stupid. If you honestly think you can maneuver more money for our investor shareholders, go ahead. But for God's sake, I'll kill you if you blow the deal or force a modification to its fairness to both sides."

"Okay."

"The moment they blink, you back off."

"Right."

I held my breath as he and his team returned to the bargaining table with Morgan Stanley.

During the week, Dick and I had more conversation, and a great deal of paper changed hands.

I'd promised them that we would show everything — the good, the bad, and the ugly.

"We will do this with total transparency," I said to Dick, "so that you can never say there was a single loan, a single document we didn't show you."

"I know, and I appreciate it he responded"

"But, in return for that, you are on notice that our situation may worsen. We both know that as the economy nose-dives, our problems compound."

"I know that. I understand that," Dick said. "And I assure you that economic deterioration is not a consideration in the pricing. We have discussed that issue, and everyone understands."

I wanted Bank of America to be aware that this was not an arrangement that was based on a moving target, and that our arrangement would have to be firm and final on the basis and exchanger terms we had put together. In essence, I wanted them to take an implied ownership from this point forward.

COMMUNICATIVE – *It is important for business leaders to know when and how to communicate critical or difficult issues.*

As if further evidence of our proliferating woes was necessary, our bank's letter of credit rating was lowered by Fitch. Again, the downgrade reflected reduced profitability prospects due to deteriorating asset quality.

I convened an emergency meeting of the executive committee of the board to update them on the progress of my discussions with Bank of America. The executive committee urged that we call the full board together and inform all the directors of how quickly talks had progressed.

The next day, while our administrative assistants scurried to set up a meeting of the board members, I received a phone call that almost blew my mind.

"Guess who?"

I couldn't believe my ears — it was Carl Reichardt. I had probably not heard from him in eight months, around the time of our aborted merger discussions. I wondered at the coincidence of his timing and concluded it was probably no coincidence. "How's it going?"

"Oh, not too bad. Say, I wonder if you and I could get together for lunch."

I stammered, "What's up? Any urgency?"

A few days before I'd signed a confidentiality agreement. I buttoned my lip. I felt my palms go sweaty.

"Nothing urgent. Just thought we ought to touch base on where we stand. I still love the benefits of in-state mergers."

"So, do I. I'd like to, but I honestly can't right now. How about September, after vacations?" Silence lingered in the air like an animal trap. He was waiting for me to say too much, to trip up, pop off, and blurt out everything. I knew that he knew. I didn't know how he knew it, and he never said he knew it, but he knew.

We set a date for late September and ended the conversation. Life was so damned peculiar. He wanted to alert me in a wordless way that he might want to get his oar in the water.

How the hell did he know? What had suddenly possessed Wells Fargo? I could only marvel at the irony. Since last December, when he had called off our merger at the last possible moment, Security Pacific credit had deteriorated. Was our institution suddenly now more appealing because Bank of America wanted to merge with us? In any event, if I was correct that his ears had perked, this was good news. Perhaps, notwithstanding our collective real estate loan exposure, Wells Fargo would be waiting in the wings if a deal with Bank of America collapsed. This would be preferable to other alternatives.

Dick and I met with our lawyers and consultant and finalized the merger agreement that was to be executed following our respective Board of Director's approvals. The Board meetings were scheduled for the following Monday, eleven days after we began these most recent discussions.

I hurried downstairs from my office to the full board meeting. The directors were surprised by the Reichardt call and because they had always favored Wells over Bank of America, they wondered if we should pursue that option. I cautioned against any further discussions, as I believed that Reichardt's effort was only an attempt to disrupt any Bank of America deal. After a full discussion, they approved the merger agreement as presented.

CAMP ROSSI WAS NO VACATION

Amid the process of working through the details of the merger, Bank of America concluded that it would be helpful to the continuity of our two banks to begin to change the culture of our bank regarding the handling of credit and loan considerations. To carry out this re-direction of the thinking process of the Security Pacific branch and head office lending personnel, a training and adjustment program was developed as a required indoctrination. I had agreed with this idea, recognizing that credit matters had not proved to be our strength, were at the root of our problems, and that we probably could use some adjustments to our thinking. I had no idea what to expect but was cautiously optimistic.

I had expressed my concerns to Dick about the unspoken growing caste system that had begun to stigmatize many of our Security Pacific employees and was making them feel unwelcome to the new organization. In response, he informed me that his Chief Credit Officer had an idea that he described as a brainstorm: he was preparing an orientation program that would not only prepare Security Pacific personnel for a transition to a stricter credit process but lay the groundwork for a more nurturing, friendly, and cooperative environment between our two bank groups. All Security Pacific managers would be expected to attend a one-day seminar to help develop this new culture.

"Bob, I'd like to baptize, as it were, the Security Pacific people in the Bank of America culture. If you agree, we'll bring every one of Security's managers into a one-day session whose purpose is to introduce and orient them, get that good-fellow feeling flowing, make them feel comfortable, ease them into the new organization, and soften the landing in this new experience."

Sounded like a solid, rational idea. "Great. How can I say no to that?"

The Bank of America Chief Credit Officer convened these summits in northern California, gathering Security Pacific managers, executives, and employees in clusters of about two hundred per session. The gatherings, we quickly heard, were nothing as represented by Rosenberg. In their reaction, our attending personnel began to label them as "Camp Rossi," named for the Bank of America's lead master of ceremonies and Chief Credit Officer. These adventures were raising the eyebrows and blood pressure of our staff, many of whom — like eyewitnesses at My Lai — seemed at a loss even to describe what they had experienced. They returned showing signs of that wartime illness, post-traumatic stress disorder.

Without going into details, one vice president phoned and left an ominous message on my voice mail. "Bob, you must check out these so called "feel good" symposiums. You'll be astounded."

I was not required or asked to attend, but I decided it was important to see what my managers were experiencing; I felt that my attendance might encourage the attendance of other executives for whom the seminar was optional.

I flew to Oakland, hopped in a rental car, and drove out to Bank of America's credit and technology facility in the East Bay. I was totally by myself and had no idea what to expect.

I grabbed a cup of coffee and entered a dim training room where Security Pacific managers lingered in apprehensive silence.

And then the pompous leader of these gatherings, the founder of the sessions, its Master of Ceremonies, attired in a green Alligator golf shirt, short pants, crisp white tennis shoes, and high white socks with a swinging coin medallion hanging around his neck, ambled through a side entrance and stepped up on the raised stage, like he had come to teach us how to mix cocktails or play tennis. He entered stage-left with a giant Styrofoam cup and a satchel crammed with handouts. The only fashion accessory missing from his apparel was a coach's whistle. I thought he was going to begin the day by ordering us to do forty push-ups. "'Morning," he muttered to the crowd. There was little response, and he addressed the group in as louder voice, as if demanding a response, "Good Morning everyone. We're going to have a great day learning the B of A way."

Following an obligatory welcome speech and abstruse introductions, he postured himself in a professorial manner and began to wander around the stage in front of his audience. In lieu of a more sociable approach, he ordered us to follow his instructions. "I want everybody in this room to raise their hands in the air," he commanded. "Raise your hands! Do it! Raise up your hands!"

With the proficiency of circus animals, we reluctantly raised our hands. A hand here, a hand there. Then ten, then forty, then two hundred. Feeling like an idiot, I raised my hands.

"You know what that is? That's you waving goodbye to your customers. Because the key to your success at Bank of America is having customers who do business with us in strict adherence to our credit policy. And my gut tells me you may have to wave goodbye to a lot of your customers."

> CONFIDENT – *Maintaining confidence in achieving the intended objective even though challenged by criticism, intimidation, and insults is significant for the business leaders.*

> DISCIPLINED – *It is important for business leaders to be disciplined in maintaining personal and human values and standards when considering or reacting to external efforts to break them.*

> COMPASSIONATE – *It is important that business leaders show empathy and compassion for the feelings of staff who are personally or professionally belittled or demeaned.*

Jesus, I thought, what sort of a routing are we in for? Where is the spirit or team building? Immediately, he tore into Security Pacific's credit methodology. "It doesn't take a John Kenneth Galbraith to see that Security Pacific is in big-time trouble. Your numbers take my breath away. I've never seen so many classified loans in my life. It's chilling."

I listened in dismay to what I hoped was a joke. Should I put a stop to this charade and perhaps put our merger at risk? I thought. Why am I just sitting here, taking this abuse? This guy must be a real nut-job.

"The answer: The Bank of America Way," he continued. "And the Bank of America Way is the only way, because it holds the secret to how we got out of our difficulties, and you will too. You are all going to learn the Bank of America Way, no exceptions. You're going to learn a new credit culture, or you're not going to be here."

A real winning approach, I thought facetiously. He wants none of our customers and none of our employees.

"Bank of America was in the same boat as you before I came over. Remember 1986? Yep—we've been there, done that, but I came in and we triumphed. We were revitalized. And you know why? Because Bank of America is a survivor. Always has been, always will be. But now times have changed, and Security Pacific is Humpty Dumpty. You've had a great fall. All the king's horses and all the king's men can't put you back together again. But I will, and Bank of America will. And if Humpty Dumpty doesn't go back together again, you're not going to work here."

An absurd chuckle from the rear of the auditorium broke the rhythm of his consciousness-raising patter.

More speeches, more insults. The orientation groaned on. Minutes flattened into hours. The second hand on my watch seemed to stop as he continued: "Is there anybody here who is opposed to the Bank of America Way? I want to hear it. Anybody?"

No one said a word.

Didn't he get it? Didn't he understand how desperately willing Security Pacific employees were to fit in? My God, we had transformed ourselves so many times, through so many permutations and strategies. Had we not demonstrated our cultural plasticity? This was like watching Wilt Chamberlain admonish Trappist monks on the topic of promiscuity.

About midway through the ordeal, I grew restless. My eyes drifted to a man in an adjacent chair. I recognized him as one of our managers — perhaps eight levels down — but I couldn't place the name. I couldn't restrain myself; I leaned over and whispered, "Can you believe this crock of bull?"

He recognized me and was surprised to hear this critique coming from the Chief Executive Officer. "Yeah, it's pretty gruesome."

"It's a damned disgrace," I whispered.

"The gap between our culture and theirs is simply not this gigantic, is it? I mean, isn't he exaggerating?"

"He's full of bull. How is this supposed to bring solidarity to these two organizations? How is this supposed to make us feel welcome?"

When he finally dismissed us, I ran. I could not get out of that room fast enough. The seminar had been interminable, the longest day of my life. When twilight descended on northern California and the prison gates opened, I thought I would have to be airlifted out by a crack team of paramedics who specialized in boredom-induced comas.

I wondered again if I should have shut him out and closed this sickening event. Why was I willing to stay silent and not protect our employees from his incendiary remarks? Was I afraid? Yes, I answered to myself. I was committed to getting this merger completed as scheduled and I didn't want to run any risk of throwing it off tracks. I knew that my staff and I must exercise control to get this job done. I had sold my soul and to some degree my leadership, for the sake of preserving value in our company for everyone.

COMMITTED – *It is important that business leaders establish and maintain a strong commitment to the resolution of select matters as well as to exercise the personal qualities required of its leaders to satisfy the mission of the company or resolve periodic issues.*

If we weren't in such trouble with only this deal as a respectable out for our investor shareholders, employees and customers, I would have told Rosenberg and all of his super-executives to go fly a kite. But I had to swallow and serve the greater purpose. I knew immediately, without deep consideration, that Security Pacific personnel would have trouble working with these new Bank of America leaders. I certainly knew that I would.

Over the next two months, some two thousand Security Pacific employees were subjected to Camp Rossi. My heart went out to them. This was so far above and beyond the call of duty that I was sorry we could not pay them some sort of emotional distress gratuity. But I was sure that they would all return to their jobs, insulted but remaining committed to seeing the resolution of our troubles to the end.

> *SELECTIVE – It is important that business leaders fairly, effectively, and selectively establish staff with resiliency and shared commitment to the expected mission.*

13

TIME IN THE WOODSHED

THE FED WANTS US DEAD

Two months after completing our merger agreement with Bank of America, my management team and I flew to San Francisco for a joint meeting with the Federal Reserve Board and other members of the regulatory community.

We arrived in San Francisco around noon for the 3:30 meeting with the collection of regulatory officials as part of a regularly scheduled review of the holding company and all subsidiaries, including the bank.

Considering our agreement and scheduled merger with Bank of America, I felt the meeting was probably unnecessary. I concluded that its purpose was to update federal regulators on the dynamics of the merger, and I naively expected them to be pleased by the fortuitous turn of events and even go so far as to perhaps congratulate us on making a deal that would save them enormous time and anguish.

When we arrived at the Federal Reserve from the airport in cabs, I was surprised to see a regulator looking for our arrival through the ground floor window, shading his eyes, glaring intently. It was obvious to me what this might be all about. He was snooping on us to see if we would arrive in deluxe limousines amid extravagant fanfare; this would be incontrovertible evidence that we were not in touch with the reality of our situation and were still living high on the hog in utter denial of our troubles.

As we entered the lobby, he greeted us and probably scanned our wrists for Rolex watches. This individual was short, pleasant, and intelligent, but I always felt he was wound too tight, even for banking. In the numerous visits I'd made to the Fed, I'd never in my life had a ground floor greeting. I felt a lump in my throat as we rose in the elevator; we were in for trouble, I was pretty sure, and I was suddenly suspicious that this would not be a positive event. There would, most likely, be no congratulations: no warm handshakes, back-slaps, flowers, award trophies, or joyful accolades.

In the conference room, we were met by a Napoleonic phalanx of regulators. We took our seats with six or seven Federal Reserve staff. Also, present were the Controller's Office lead examiner, his staff, and an examiner from the Federal Deposit Insurance Corporation. The mood was initially cordial but quickly turned dour, more appropriate to the viewing of a dignitary lying in state than to a regulatory review. After perfunctory introductions, the meeting began.

We had also prepared and intended to make a presentation, but before we could begin, the Federal Reserve regulator who met us downstairs began to speak and, in so doing, set the tone. "Gentlemen, we've painstakingly reviewed and re-reviewed your bank and the holding company and have concluded that your bank continues to deteriorate."

No kidding, I thought. Good detective work, Sherlock!

He continued. "Your deterioration continues such that we now feel that you absolutely must make a concerted effort to increase the level of your capital to support these increasingly criticized loans."

Good God, I thought, as the meeting took on the absurdity of a Flannery O'Connor story. Did this man live in a cave? Didn't he read the newspapers or watch TV? Hadn't he heard the news? We had signed a definitive agreement to merge with Bank of America less than two months prior. With some wonderment I said, "I think you should be aware that we just did raise capital."

UNDERSTAND PRACTICES AND STANDARDS – Remaining aware of the standards and norms of the regulatory community is an important leadership quality.

FINANCIAL UNDERSTANDING – It is important for business leaders to be financially capable to understand the implications of accounting, tax, investment, and financial transactions.

"You just raised capital?"

I felt like saying, Sure, dipshit, about $6 billion, but I held my tongue. "As I'm sure you are aware, we have a merger agreement with the Bank of America."

"The merger?"

Wait a minute, I thought, these guys can't possibly be this stupid. Something else had to be going on here. "Yes, the merger. Capital is the point of the merger agreement. We want to merge with Bank of America, an institution that has a lot of capital. That is my solution to our capital weakness. We intend to combine a company without a lot of capital with a company with a lot of capital and, consequently, enhance our capital."

"I understand that, "he said, "but what if the merger doesn't take place for some reason or another?"

"We have an agreement that can only be broken in the event of a Material Adverse Change, which is the only out or condition specified in the agreement. Bank of America has thoroughly reviewed our assets. Believe me, they've seen everything. I feel relatively safe in saying that, barring some act of God, we have successfully raised capital by merging with the best-capitalized bank around."

He glanced at his associates at the Fed. Then he returned his gaze to me. "Merger aside, we still believe Security Pacific has to raise capital."

I glanced at my team in dismay, then looked back. "Maybe I'm missing something. I don't understand the logic." Under our current circumstances, new capital would be hard to come by and very expensive. If I could have plucked capital out of my ears like violets out of a bouquet I would have done so. "Can you give me one solid reason why the merger won't happen?"

"Because you don't have enough capital."

I felt like I was trying to explain trigonometry to a turnip. "That is why we're doing the merger — to get capital. Bank of America fully recognizes our financial status and they want to go forward."

The humidity in the room seemed to levitate in direct proportion to the rising tension. Our greeter's neck turned bright red, as it often did when he became irritated. "But what if there are complications?"

"I can't imagine what could go wrong under the circumstances, but if that should occur then we will raise capital, and you probably won't have me to kick around anymore because I'll be gone. Let me add parenthetically, if you want to kill this merger deal, force us to raise capital. I don't think you want to be responsible for the collapse of this deal, do you?" I looked around the table for some inkling of recognition, some comprehension of the truth I was speaking. I saw nothing.

He sighed; his neck continued to brighten, approaching the hue of a Jalapeño pepper. "If the deal falls through, then what will you do about capital?"

"If the merger doesn't happen, and I have every reason to believe it will, then we'll raise capital."

"How?"

"We'll create a contingency strategy so that, in the event the deal falls apart, we have a plan to raise capital. Will that alleviate your concerns?"

He looked at his superiors, then turned back to the Security Pacific team. "Sounds good." Then he threw us another curve. "Notwithstanding the fact we accept your plan to give us a plan on how you would raise capital if this deal falls through, we feel you should further augment your loan loss reserves."

"Pardon me?" I cocked my head in disbelief. I thought I heard a couple of my associates gasps.

"We feel it is essential that you significantly increase your reserve for loan losses in view of the continuing deterioration of your loan portfolio and the increases in your criticized assets."

Once again, he was making no sense. Many of my staff shook their heads, stared down at the table. I hardly knew what to say. "Let me get this straight. You want me to arbitrarily move a large amount of money into reserves, at this point? After we've signed a merger agreement?"

He nodded in response.

"If we don't increase capital, and our protection is the capital and the reserves, what honest-to-god difference does it make whether the money is in the capital account or the reserve account? The net result is the same."

"Well, I know, but we want to see it in the reserve account."

"You want me to shuffle money into reserves so that you can remind the world what a big problem we have. This is a regulator-sanctioned exercise in self-humiliation, is that right?"

He shrugged.

"You recognize, I'm sure, that Security Pacific is a public corporation and, as such, is a regulated institution that publicly reports its financial status on an ongoing basis and whose reserve adequacy methodologies were long ago blessed not only by our accountants but by you and other regulators. Now for me to arbitrarily move funds from the capital account to the reserve for loan losses account could make it look like we are publicly misrepresenting the status of the company."

"We want considerably more reserves, in case the deal falls through."

That's not what he wants, I thought. He wants me to look like a bumbling idiot. I carefully tried to articulate the paradox of what they were asking me to do. "Respectfully, this makes no sense. You're asking me to take money out of my right-hand pocket and put it into my left-hand pocket."

"Will you do as we ask?"

"I will promise only that we will review our methodologies. Rest assured, we will do only what is appropriate to maintain the integrity and accurate reporting of the balance sheet of our corporation."

One of the federal regulators piped up: "What do you mean by that?"

"I mean, honest to God, we have an adequate level of reserves based on our methodology. To shift that kind of money arbitrarily will bring a lawsuit."

"What do you mean, lawsuit?"

"The shareholders will think we've been dishonest. And you know Wall Street has ears.

If a stock analyst reads that we've suddenly slid a billion dollars into reserves, he goes to Bank of America and says, 'What the hell are you doing, are you crazy, buying a piece of crap like Security Pacific?' The rumor mill starts churning and then Bank of America's stock drops. This will have huge repercussions. There must be some rationale to your madness. I must be intellectually honest with the investors on the street who are going to wonder why in the hell I would put one nickel more into reserves than our methodology requires. It's going to be mighty hard to explain why I'm mindlessly shoving a big hunk of money into reserves after I've cut a merger deal with one of the best-capitalized banks in the world. If we go along with you on this, any fallout is your responsibility."

After a few more detailed points and comments, the meeting concluded with my promise to the Federal Reserve to come up with a plan to raise capital if the merger should fall through.

Their message was loud and clear: Mr. Smith, you have screwed up this bank and now you must pay.

THE CONSPIRACY THEORY

One matter was always obvious to us. While it may take some time, regulators will not forget and will work constantly to get even for words or actions that disrespect them individually or as a group. They seemed to hold revenge in their hearts for those who failed to meet their expectations for response to their wishes. When you got on their bad list, you could not rest until they saw that the playing field had been leveled.

Our history in showing respect was horrendous and had been led for years by our prior CEO, who on numerous occasions had issued open insults for the regulatory work and findings. This attitude was reflected in many segments of our company, and it wasn't long before we got on their "hit" list and were tagged as an uncooperative and unpleasant company.

As the merger progressed and our problems continued, I had personally become the focus of the regulatory group with respect to our company's disrespect for them as well as our escalating problems. I knew I had the responsibility and was willing to stand personally accountable, even though I had assumed most of the situation and managed the bank to remedy a lot of what had gone wrong. But I knew that, even so, I had been a part of it all.

> ACCOUNTABLE – *It is important that business leaders assume accountability for whatever actions they have perpetrated or participated in during their job tenure.*

Through many conversations directly with me and my staff I had also become cognizant that the executive team of Bank of America was aware of our regulatory reputation. I also knew that many of the B of A team felt that they could be shut out in their efforts to assume higher positions in the surviving organization with a leadership change away from Bank of America executives. They had concluded that they were better, more capable, and superior, while we were reckless and inferior, as was made clear in the Camp Rossi debacle. They felt that this entitled them to greater opportunities, and they didn't want anything or person standing in the way.

They were also cognizant of the merger agreement details in which I had been anointed as the successor to Rosenberg. I was sure they all felt that such a decision was grossly undeserved and would negatively impact each of their personnel career opportunities. I was told that this subject was part of regular water cooler conversations between a few of Bank of America's management and the lead examiner. Rosenberg was often put on the spot about why, under all the circumstances, this was permitted and the impact it might have on the company. This talk was passed on to Rosenberg who, perhaps, shared their feelings but knew that he must deal with the matter in order to maintain the continued support of his executives and the lead examiner. I was told that he had discussed the issue with the lead examiner, and they had collectively concluded or colluded, perhaps for differing reasons, that I should never be permitted to lead the company.

The decision and timing of being informed that my potential succession would no longer be acknowledged or accepted was more than coincidental. I was told by Rosenberg and the next day by the lead examiner that this was a decision for the benefit and in the best interests of everyone. They both used the same explanation. They had cut a deal that achieved some regulatory retribution and satisfied the concerned Bank of America executives. Rosenberg was willing to take the chance that I would not revolt, want the deal canceled, or seek concessions in response to this decision.

A clear knife in the back had been constructed by both the regulators and the Bank of America executives; however, this decision was personally not important or relevant to me or what I really wanted. My reaction was to not take it too personally but instead remain focused on getting the deal done.

DISCIPLINED - It is important that business leaders remain disciplined, acting with dignity and composure, when addressing negative issues or situations.

I assume they all got what they wanted, but I don't think they realized that I would remain so adamantly focused on getting what I wanted as well: a rewarding resolution for the investor shareholders, customers, and most employees and peace of mind for the work we had accomplished.

14

GOVERNMENT DEMANDS

OUR BOARD IS PUT ON THE SPOT

The one thing we didn't need as we moved through the necessary elements of the merger agreement was increased intervention and exploration of our troubles under a mandate from the regulators. But our hopes to move on without their involvement were not realized, once the lead regulator formally requested that our board appoint a special committee to investigate the causal chain of events leading to Security Pacific's decline. At my suggestion, our board had already chartered such a study a few days prior, so perhaps the regulator got wind of this action and was just jumping on the bandwagon, or the fact that both groups were moving in the same direction was just a coincidence.

"What we want," he explained, repeating virtually word for word my thoughts expressed at our board meeting a few days prior, "is a special study committee. This would be an independent collection of observers who would conduct a fact-finding mission and issue a report to the Board enumerating the causes and factors contributing to the decline of the bank. Why the deterioration? What, or who, was to blame?" They had stolen our thoughts to ensure their inclusion in this important examination. We wanted to know what had gone wrong, and why, encouraging the board to undertake this analysis.

The timing and subtext of this study, along with the regulator's formal request, put me under additional pressure. I had no idea how long this investigation would take or how it might impact the merger. The inference from the regulators — that blame had to be located and apportioned —was unfriendly. Nevertheless, it was important to play ball with the regulators in order to keep moving forward. If the results were what I anticipated, I hoped this would be an opportunity for me to clean the slate with the regulators personally. "I see no problem," I told them. "I will meet with our board of directors next Tuesday and suggest that your specific requests, especially those related to fixing blame, be included in the study we have already chartered. I will get their thoughts and obtain their approval to move forward and meet your request."

"What sort of time frame are we talking about?" I asked our top regulator.

"Don't you think a month or two would be sufficient?"

I didn't know. An investigation like this — examining events that occurred years before — could take a significant amount of time. The pressure was on to do it quickly, and this made me nervous, but the board undertook the challenge with seriousness and full commitment to submit their report within thirty days, if for no other reason than to keep the regulators happy and at bay.

Moving very quickly and joined by several well-paid banking experts and consultants, the special study committee was prepared to render its opinion after an examination of the prevailing facts, findings, and history of the bank's deterioration. The appointed committee chairperson, who was responding within the suggested thirty days, reviewed the findings at a meeting of the committee followed the next day by a meeting with a collection of representatives from the bank's regulating bodies.

"In accordance with the direction of the bank's senior management and the regulatory agencies, we as a board committee, working with a strong group of professional banking experts and consultants, conducted a full investigation of the deterioration, its causes and origins. We have a pretty good understanding of what happened and why."

Our committee member summarized roughly five years of our bank's activities, focusing specifically on the Merchant Bank and our real estate lending practices. "Throughout this period, the bank embarked on a very aggressive program to augment earnings. Prior to the recent recession, its credit culture was by all appearances aligned with successful policy. Credit quality ratings remained strong until the beginning of this decade. When the economy slumped, there was serious and quick erosion in the real estate market. Compounded by the effects of FIRREA, the consequences to the bank's loan portfolio were profound. Throughout this deterioration, management took substantial and vigorous actions to counteract these forces and the board backed these efforts. This corrective process has continued, despite the planned merger and further attempts to remedy, the deterioration are ongoing. This includes the dismantling of the Merchant Bank, expense cuts, elimination of executive bonuses, and many other steps."

"We found no instances of fraud, negligence, or abuse," our committee member continued. "The corporation has a strong, entrepreneurial bent, and its scope is multifaceted, diversified, and broad. The strategies, including the formation of the Merchant Bank, while ambitious, were slow in developing and experienced considerable drawbacks during the hard economic times.

"While mistakes were made, no one at the bank sat down one night and concocted a scheme to immerse the bank in risk that might jeopardize its future. This committee can pinpoint no specific action, individual, or instance and say, 'This was wrong, this was the cause of the fall.'

The cause of the decline was due to an agglomeration of events. The reasons previously given for the bank's hardship are in fact the reasons for its descent. There is no sleight of hand going on here. Furthermore, when problems were detected, the reaction was swift, proactive, and what could be expected from competent management and board action. No one was asleep at the switch. Motives were above board, and there were no executives trying to figure out how to feather their nests at the expense of the larger corporation."

Thank God, I thought. This was what I had hoped and prayed for.

The committee chairperson concluded the formal portion of the report. "This predicament was the result of a complex series of circumstances, some within and some beyond the control of senior management. The bank had lower capital ratios, poor funding, and depleted reserves entering this recessionary period. Of the California major banks, our bank was the most at risk. Remember, there is currently a lot going on in the outfield: Working with the board, the bank staff is continuing to perform tirelessly in resolving and collecting many defaulted real estate loans and the challenges of dismantling the Merchant Bank."

He concluded his report. "The deterioration is symptomatic of what we saw in the 1980s, when all the banks followed each other. The actions senior management took were in general concordance with the culture and climate of the time. Questions? Comments?"

I waited.

The lead examiner seemed unusually dispirited by the good news. "But the board didn't change," he argued.

The Chairperson paused. "What do you mean, sir?"

"The responsibility has to be shared with the board."

"What?"

The regulator lifted his voice. "I'm critical of the board and the continuing arrogance of management in not accepting the full accountability for these problems."

Another committee member, a former U.S. ambassador and now a director on the board, jumped in. "I have a different perspective. As a real estate developer, I've seen firsthand the living hell this economy has inflicted on California. I'm very happy this study was done — it is indispensable, as it sheds light on what is becoming a New World both in real estate and in California. And while I'm saddened, I don't feel this board has any reason to feel ashamed."

The regulator sat far back in his chair, uncharacteristically silent.

I thanked the chairperson and the committee. "I appreciate this discussion a lot, and I think we've learned something from this report and hopefully we can apply these lessons and become a better organization. But I dislike the aspersions being cast around, particularly at the board. I'm the guy at the top and I'm accountable. I admit there was arrogance on our part, but I don't feel it was ever personal or mean-spirited and certainly is not evident today. As far as our current weakness, I think the merger is the solution. If all goes well, we should have a very satisfactory outcome and end up with a very sound bank."

ACCOUNTABLE - Business leaders must be willing to assume accountability for the company's actions and results.

CONFIDENT - Responding with confidence in achieving the intended objective is an important leadership quality when challenged by criticism, intimidation, and insults.

Then I turned to the regulator, "any comments?"

He roused himself out of a melancholy stupor. "My conclusion remains the same. As I see it, the management team is inferior. Board oversight is insufficient. As for the merger, it is certainly the way out of this mess. But what do we have when it's over? Management walks away with clean hands."

"Whoa, whoa. I don't intend to walk away from anything." On the contrary, I saw myself as walking from one storm into a very challenging atmosphere.

"And the board walks away clean; their jobs go on; their careers go on."

> *UNDERSTAND PRACTICES AND STANDARDS – It is important that business leaders establish cooperation, communication, and understanding with industry and regulatory authorities. It is important to stay informed and maintain a positive, constructive relationship with these parties.*

He had apparently not heard what he wanted to hear. I hoped, but doubted, that this report would soften the approach he would take going forward and dissuade or at least neutralize his criticism of our bank and its management and board.

THE BAD REVIEWS CONTINUE

While I was defensive of our work, I also knew that many of our troubled loans were out of line with disciplined quality-oriented credit leadership. As I proceeded through this difficult period, I was often reminded of personal experiences that caused me to question our credit culture and aggressive attraction to real estate developers during the last few years of the decade. Many of these loans were made secured by properties that would eventually be negatively impacted by the appraisal policies mandated by FIRREA; yet they still were the result of our aggressive real estate loan strategies and policies.

About a year prior to our serious troubles I had personally reviewed our problem real estate related loans in economically depressed Arizona. We had a long list of properties that were either not preforming or where the developer had just given us back the keys. I focused on the top ten of these problems and decided I would personally visit the site of these projects to get a better feeling as to why the property valuations were so depressed and why so many of these loans were being written down to a level that could not be supported by reduced (even pre-FIRREA) appraised values.

After flying to the state on a very warm spring day, my first visit was to a rural shopping center that was in default, as the owners were not even paying interest on the loan. This center also had missed its construction budget and needed more money to ensure completion. While the Phoenix area development and growth had previously been moving at a fast pace, new jobs and in-migration had now suddenly stopped. No new homes were under development; only streets, utilities, and partially developed properties were in evidence.

This neighborhood shopping center was only 30% occupied, with a multitude of "For Lease" signs evident in many of the spaces. We had a $9 million loan against an original $18 million property appraisal and not enough remaining cash to build out leasehold improvements or to sustain care of the project. As it stood that day, the best opinion of the appraiser was that it would take ten years to be fully viable generating a positive cash flow. It was his view that we could perhaps sell the project on an "as is" basis for about $3 million. It was clear that there would be no market for this property nor would there be any buyer interest on a fully valued basis for several years. As I stood talking to the developer, I could see several sage-brush bundles being blown through the project and driven over the barren undeveloped home lots on three sides of the project.

We then stopped by a beautiful 30-acre residential development in Camelback, a community outside Phoenix. Four model homes had been developed along with the roads, offsite improvements, and utilities for about sixty more homes. Nothing else was going on that might support our $15 million loan on a project that was initially appraised at $30 million. Our best guess was that an "as is" sale might realize $3 to $5 million. But again, there was no line of interested buyers. Only the vultures circled the development were in evidence.

These examples were repeated in the other eight projects we viewed. This was clearly a disaster that would cost us millions of dollars. I wondered why we had made these loans without considering the direction of the economy or the ability to have other sources of repayment. We had failed to execute traditionally accepted credit principles in what now looked like a banking disaster. And at this moment, we hadn't yet seen or felt the impact of FIRREA.

In another example of our failures, we had a large Orange County developer who was having cash flow short-falls in his home development projects. The sale of his developed homes was slowing, putting severe pressure on his operations which included a number of other projects. To help this situation and because we had additional credit extended to this borrower, we made a seventy-five-million-dollar loan secured by his home and exotic and antique car collection. We hoped that this loan would rectify his cash flow issues and be a bridge to adjusting his overall business effort.

The lead examiners began an examination of our larger real estate loans and selected this bridge loan for their examination. After two weeks they examiner told us the loan was a loss. They wanted the loan charged off immediately, even before the first interest payment was due and even though it was well secured. When I questioned this conclusion, the regulators responded that this decision was intended as a message to all banks not to bail out developers from their cash flow shortfalls. They were taking a hard stand, and the reality was that these loans were naively made and poorly thought through. It was obvious that in an economic downturn our real estate related loans would severely impact the developers as well as our bank for several years.

We had sought every real estate developer to be our customer and, in the process, we had produced a lot of trouble by our aggressive strategies. We wanted to outgrow the competition and in the process had not sufficiently considering the changing economic conditions. We had become too bold and aggressive and had not properly accounted for the possibility that we could be seriously impacted by a stressed economic environment.

PROTECTIVE - The best response of leadership to adversity and unexpected events is to be protective in establishing and maintaining quality standards.

I had quickly become aware that while I was not fully innocent of leadership failures, there were significant areas and matters that had slipped by our disciplines. Many, now troubled, loans had passed because of the momentum and efforts undertaken to expand our business interests, and to beat out our competitors, particularly in real estate lending. We had sought to take advantage of the good times and growth experienced in most of the decade. In so doing, we had mistakenly relied on anticipated continued growth, particularly in California, where the economic history over the past fifty plus years had failed to show significant weaknesses. We had not properly planned for the eventual economic decline and the fact that good times don't last forever.

15

A REAL CRISIS

TROUBLE FROM AN ERISA PROBLEM

About four months prior to the intended closing of the merger, a routine regulatory examination of our New York-based securities activities reported that the unit had a violation of the Employee Retirement Income Security Act, or ERISA, as it is known. The ERISA rules were designed to protect pension schemes from activities that could cause financial damage to pension participants. Our New York activity had initiated arrangements with pension schemes to enhance the potential return on their holding of U.S. government securities as part of our repo/reverse repo operation. This was the same activity that sought the Japanese institution's holdings of government securities.

I understood the legality of the matters noted and had turned a review of the issues of our risk of exposure over to our Chief Legal Counsel. He had subsequently employed two outside legal experts to get us the best advice possible. After two weeks of examination, they advised us that while there was no exposure to the regulatory noted violation, they had discovered that we had most likely violated another provision of ERISA for very complex debatable technical reasons. Their major concern was the interpretation of the defined form of violation as it applied to the penalties stipulated in the regulations. After further review and discussions with outside counsel, we met on this matter to be sure it wouldn't potentially impact our pending merger. After a closer look, both our inhouse counsel and the outside attorneys believed they had a full grasp of the ERISA violations and the potential penalties. I had spoken with them recently, but something in their voices did not evoke confidence.

I felt this matter would not amount to a great deal since the discovery was the result of our own independent work and not a regulatory finding.

They cascaded into my office, each man hauling a pull cart of documents, files, folders, and reports. Halfway kidding, I said, "So what are the penalties? Are 45,000 of our people going to be out on the street with empty soup cans?"

The lead outside attorney answered with seriousness: "That depends, and I do mean that literally. Your question is rhetorical, but there is more truth there than you could possibly know."

The attorneys were in no mood for frivolity.

I shivered a bit at their response and continuing dour faces.

We continued as our Chief Legal Counsel lit a cigarette, paused to enjoy the feeling of smoke in his lungs, and gazed out the window at a nearby skyscraper. "Just to fast forward to your initial comment," he noted, "the answer to that question could be decided relative not only to the amount of the transactions but also the number of the transactions over several years. You know there are billions of dollars and tens of thousands of transactions."

"Yes, but what does that potentially mean in dollars?" I'd prepared myself mentally for the possibility of a potential $50 million penalty. But that was my worse-case scenario.

He waved his cigarette. It was his style to deliver bad news with the warm smile and engaging countenance of a favorite grandfather.

"Unfortunately, this potential misuse of pension funds is not something that they just thought up this year. The records reflect that this process that is being challenged began nearly seven years ago."

I heard a sick laugh.

"No," he said, "this constitutes, unfortunately, not one seven-year transaction, but thousands of multi-million-dollar one-night transactions over the seven-year period."

"I want to make sure I understand," I gulped. "Not only are we potentially liable for what we did in 1991, we are theoretically liable for every overnight transaction dating all the way back to 1984? How can that be? We're the ones who discovered the violation."

"That's about the size of it," he said.

I thought, this can't possibly be happening. My customary optimism gave way to a siege of negative thoughts, visions, and nightmare hallucinations. It felt unreal. "So, this is a real big problem and not my imagination?" I shook my head. "Christ, that could be billions of transaction dollars."

He nervously exhaled smoke and said calmly, "It's a potential catastrophe."

The fact that these practices were now in question but had been routine since 1984 begged the question: Where was everybody? Not only had our internal accountants and auditors missed it, but the Federal Reserve, who'd audited this unit several times, had never mentioned, flagged, or even questioned the transactions. As recently as August, the Federal Reserve had again reviewed our practices and had not noted this as a problem.

"We conducted a full analysis from the end of 1984 to May of 1991, when they ceased this practice. There was a cumulative $570 billion of these business transactions."

"Of that amount," I asked, "what was the involvement of pension account participation?"

"Roughly $12.7 billion."

"We now estimate the stipulated potential penalty or excise tax on the ERISA-related transactions to be approximately $672 million if the transactions are held to be prohibitive sales or are determined to be within the definition of self-dealing."

I didn't even register that number; it flew into my head and right out again. "Then let me ask, are they sales? Are we positive they were sales?"

"You see, you've put your finger on the crux of the problem. How these transactions are defined is the single most important determining factor on how badly we are penalized. The transactions might be sales, or loans, or use of funds."

"Whatever they are defined, what kind of penalties are we talking about?"

"In the best of all possible worlds, these transactions were rudimentary, nearly automated, short-term use or loan of funds. In that case, the penalty may be in the $300,000 range. But if in fact these transactions are deemed to be overnight sales, the potential ERISA penalty is much higher. The total penalty would be about a billion dollars, including the accumulative interest costs and potential excise tax."

"You mean a million-dollar penalty."

"No, billion—with a B."

No. That can't be right. A billion dollars? Guys, that's about 25% of our capital! A billion dollars? What for? We didn't benefit from the transactions; the customer received the benefit. I'm sure we didn't do it on purpose. It's technical, it's complex, and it was an oversight."

I still didn't really believe what I had just heard. Really, I thought, that can't be right. He means a million.

Good, good God, I thought.

CONFIDENT – During the most stressful times the tendency of business leaders is to let emotions take charge rather than exhibiting calm and confident leadership as the preferred response.

FEARLESS – During the most stressful times, it is important for business leaders to respond without fear, effectively conveying to both staff and affiliate groups that the situation can be effectively resolved.

LEGAL AWARENESS– Maintaining an understanding of legal issues and their potential impact on the company is an important element to effective leadership.

"Bolstering our assertion that we didn't engage in these transactions intentionally is the fact that there were two separate operations utilizing pension accounts in the transaction of overnight funds; one of them did it perfectly correctly, obtained all the necessary approvals. The other function did it wrong. If, in the end, the unauthorized transactions are defined as sales, this situation could be a flat out disaster!" Our Chief Legal Counsel had an unusual quality of voice; if I wasn't looking at him, I'd have thought he was jolly.

I asked them how we had defined these transactions to our customers.

"In our accounting statements, we characterized these transactions in writing—as sales, not as a loan or a use of funds."

"You mean, if I'm hearing you correctly, if these transactions are deemed to be individual sales, we essentially violated ERISA gazillions of times every single day for several hundred weeks?"

"Yes, and keep in mind that the statutory penalty for improper transactions is 5% of the amount of the transaction."

I said nothing for a minute or two. "We have to present our case. Who do we make our case to?"

He answered with a diplomatic serenity that was beginning to irritate me. "The Controller's Office, the Federal Reserve, Department of Labor and, in the end, the statue set out that the Internal Revenue Service has final jurisdiction over the penalties. The IRS calls the shots, but we have to play to all these constituents."

"So, our best shot is to persuade the IRS that this was a loan or use of funds and not a sale?"

"That would keep the penalty down to a very understandable $300,000. You see, the 5% of each transaction penalty formula under ERISA provisions will apply to each individual transaction in the event these are deemed sales. That's where we really get whacked."

Still doubting the billion-dollar figure, I mentally applied the 5% penalty formula to $12.7 billion. "If these are deemed to be sales, by my calculation the penalty would be $672 million."

"You got it," he said "You see now that this is a veritable disaster. Now add to that number a litany of interest charges for the many years and ancillary penalties." He now balanced his cigarette on the armrest and showed me the matrix of data calculations that confirmed the numbers.

Instantaneously three words flashed in my mind: Material Adverse Change. This was the one provision to the deal that would permit Bank of America to back out without serious harm to their standing or position. This was the provision I confirmed to the Federal Reserve would never happen other than by an act of God. I hoped that this wasn't God speaking.

Bank of America was no fool. They might want Security Pacific and might even want it badly— but not this badly. No way. For all the happy-go-lucky lip service Rosenberg paid to our deteriorated credit, reserves, and quarterly losses; he would have to be brain-dead or a masochist to go forward with us knowing he could eventually face a billion-dollar penalty.

Our Chief Legal Counsel added, "There is another way that this ERISA business could disrupt the merger. Any resolution or finalization of the issues could take months. As you know, our closing date is just a month or two away. It is likely that hashing out this predicament could take at least six months, maybe a year or longer. Our deterioration will continue. And as you know, Bank of America has the option to pull out of the deal in the event they declare a MAC clause or in any event in six months, which would be September of this year, if we are unable to close the transaction."

I had a pounding headache.

"So," He continued, "this could unseat the merger like nothing else we could have imagined."

A potential billion-dollar violation? A six-month dick dance with the Internal Revenue Service? Our stock price dropping to $4 a share? Bank of America pulling out of the deal in disgust? The shareholders would hunt me down with torches, spears, and axes; they would hoist me from a Security Pacific sign.

"What do you think of this, Bob?" he asked. "What is your plan?"

"My plan? I'm going to drop by the magic shop, get a fake goatee and mustache, withdraw several hundred dollars from the bank, and purchase a one-way ticket to Israel where there's no extradition."

He lifted his hands. "Let's not panic."

"Why not?" I asked seriously.

"I'm going to talk to the regulators and see if they have any ideas on how we can push this through the obstacle course. It's the IRS I'm most concerned about."

All right, I thought, don't panic. "We need to gather all the information."

"I'm going to sit down and write a comprehensible and compelling argument that these transactions were not sales but a reasonable and logical use of funds, even though we have typified them on the documentation as sales. Then I'll solicit third-party opinions to validate that conclusion."

"We'll augment our support as we go. If we can convince the Controller's Office in Washington, they'll speak up for us and help convince the Fed, and the Fed will support our conclusion with the Department of Labor. It's a daisy chain of hope and conviction."

"But," I said, "spring-boarding off what you said, this could take eons. However, it could work because if our Bank of America deal fails they will all have an even bigger problem trying to stabilize and recapitalize our bank."

"Well, it could but it can't. We won't allow it." Like a mysterious magician he stood up, gathered his papers, and walked out of the office. He made a phone call to Price Waterhouse; asking them to prepare an independent review and opinion on the definition of our transactions.

Within three weeks, after numerous meetings and discussions, we had three hurdles behind us, convincing (with considerable pain and expressions of disgust on their part) the Controller's Office, the Federal Reserve and the Department of Labor. But the biggest hurdle remained; unquestionably the last and most onerous effort lay ahead. We had not only to present but to resolve the ERISA issue with the IRS in the two weeks remaining before the intended closing or the merger could be a dead duck. I thought about how hard it was to get the IRS to answer the phone in two weeks.

Although the legal staff had been successful with the bank regulators, which was familiar turf, they were increasingly reluctant to enter the ring with an unfamiliar opponent like the Internal Revenue Service.

"I'm having second thoughts." Our Chief Legal Counsel noted as he shook his head in a rare gesture of insecurity. "We've done well so far, we have honest to God momentum, but prodding the IRS to reach a decision on this complex an issue in two weeks is going to be harder than trying to get regulators to be pleasant. I simply don't think I have the political ammunition to get them off their ass. Deadlines mean nothing to the IRS."

I was sympathetic to the expressed plight but had no solution. "I can't think of any alternative to just going in and making our case."

"There is one narrow but incandescent ray of hope."

"Don't keep me in suspense."

"My idea is to find some Washington-based attorney who knows his way around this thick-headed bureaucracy."

"I like it. Go inject some beltway know-how into this matter. You have my carte blanche to do whatever — and I mean whatever — it takes to get this resolved."

Three days later he phoned from Washington, D.C. to relay his success. "I think I've found 'The Man.' He is a former Commissioner of the Internal Revenue Service. He's going to bat for us."

"Wow." What a genius, I thought. Can he do all this in two weeks?"

"He believes he can. He's very well connected. And I'm told the IRS staff people trust him implicitly."

When I heard this, I was struck mute. How had we gotten him on our side? I didn't analyze how it was done, I just thanked God our Chief Legal Counsel had come to work for Security Pacific.

"There is also something more. Not only does he know his way around the IRS, but he honestly agrees 100% with our interpretation of the transactions."

"No question," I said. "Send him in there with my blessing."

"But there is one small catch on all this that I must tell you," my counsel continued. I told him that if he got it resolved in two weeks we would pay him a million dollars for that success."

"Perfect," I said. "That ought to really get him going and finally get us out of trouble. We must get this deal done."

One week before the merger was set to close, the ERISA issue was finally settled in a formal agreement. The Controller's Office fined us $50,000 for false reporting and the Internal Revenue Service leveled a penalty of $239,349 and we paid our Washington attorney $1 million for his efforts.

At our San Francisco Bank of America management meeting that week we made them aware of the penalty without giving them a lot of specifics or details and did not mention the potential "B" word or the commitment to our Washington attorney. The executive who ran Camp Rossi went out of his way to put our nose in the dirt by chastising us for our stupidity and lack of oversight on this matter. We stayed quiet because we knew we were so close to the end.

The same Bank of America officer then went on to detail a $40 million penalty that had been assessed against them for faulty securities transfers related to a client in London. Keeping silent and like a child in school, I passed a note to one of my staff in the meeting that said, "Who is Stupid Now?"

PUTTING MY CAREER ON THE LINE

As we foraged our way through the troubles and uncertainties associated with getting the deal closed and before the ERISA issue was resolved, I became well aware of the depth of the uncertainties and the ability Bank of America had to pull out if the ERISA deal became a prolonged or costly issue. I purposely decided not to inform Bank of America at any point about the possibility of an ultimate billion-dollar penalty or the million-dollar commitment made to our Washington IRS attorney. Why would I want them to get their nose into knowing about or resolving this problem? My experience with them and their attitude toward us suggested that this would not be helpful. They would over-think and over-work the issue and probably piss off our Washington attorney. I felt I had no obligation to them since it was our issue, and I was the one responsible for its resolution.

We had a Material Adverse Change clause in our agreement, but we became cognizant that the terms lacked definition or any certainty that an event would or would not be defined by a court as material enough to allow Bank of America to pull out of the agreement. If they were to make such a claim we could expect a significant delay in the closing, most likely past the September cancellation date, putting the merger's completion at great risk.

ETHICAL – There are times when business leaders can be expected to keep certain information on important matters from others and still exercise minimal ethical values. Offering full disclosure and being totally transparent can often make resolution or solution of complex issues more difficult and potentially harm the company.

I knew that in either case our company would be facing a serious threat of either failure or seizure of the bank by the regulators and result in a substantial loss and a prolonged period of chaos among the employees. There would be no hope in salvaging value without new capital and a change of leadership. In most cases it would be next to impossible to get new capital without new leadership that held the trust of both the investor community and the regulatory bodies.

I realized that if the deal with Bank of America failed for any reason it would be necessary for the board to act quickly making the changes necessary to salvage the interests held by both the investor shareholders and the employees.

We held our regular board meeting in December in the middle of all the ERISA uncertainty and the continuing loan troubles; the latter had continued to grow in the failing economy.

After opening the board meeting by giving them an update on the situation and an overview of the chances for failure or delay of the deal, which I saw as about 50%. I added my suggested actions for the board if

Bank of America for whatever reason declared a Material Adverse Change or if the deal was significantly delayed for any reason.

"Gentlemen and Ladies, I am going to ask you to fire me immediately if the deal fails or is significantly delayed. This deal is our only immediate hope for our shareholders and employees. If the deal doesn't close, my leadership fails, and I must be replaced for you to effectively manage the recovery and keep the bank out of the hands of the regulators. You must have new leadership and be able to attract new capital to support the company's existence. I would suggest you think about how both could be immediately accomplished. New leadership will have to come from outside the bank and be someone who will command the confidence of both Wall Street and the regulators. I am willing to leave without conflict to the company but note that under these circumstances, time will be of the essence. Most likely one of you will have to assume temporary leadership for a period until the new leadership and capital issues can be rectified."

The next week I made application for an increased loan on my residence, knowing that if I left, I would be unemployable in the industry for some time. Having given up my source of income and having lost most of the value in my stock ownership plus all the value of my vested options, I would need cash to survive.

The press release arrived via fax on Monday, March 23, three weeks before the ERISA issue was formally resolved, on Federal Reserve letterhead which read:

"The Federal Reserve Board today approved the application of Bank of America Corporation, San Francisco, to merge with Security Pacific Corporation, Los Angeles, and thereby acquire Security Pacific's banking and non-banking subsidiaries." The deal would get done, and I would not be fired provided the ERISA issue could be satisfactorily resolved over these last few weeks.

16

REVENGE OF THE NERDS

OUR REGULATOR DUMPS ON US

Three weeks before the merger with Bank of America closed was Black Tuesday, as I would come to think of it. This was the day of our semi-annual review by the lead regulator representing the Comptroller's Office. The report was scheduled to review findings and criticisms pertaining to the last half of 1991 and the first few weeks of 1992.

From a historical perspective and as discussed earlier, we had never had a warm or constructive relationship with our primary regulator. We had little respect for the regulators and generally considered their work to be unwanted and of little value, although required. We routinely had made fun of them, both as a group and individually, often arguing vehemently over their findings and criticisms. What they saw as black, we saw as white. We saw them as a bunch of newly graduated college nerds trying to direct us, as the star athletes.

This attitude obviously didn't do us well given our recent failings and troubles, and like any group that was unfairly suppressed, the nerds wanted revenge and now it was time to repay us for treating them as a nuisance to our business.

The lead examiner and his three assistants met us, as scheduled, in a conference room on the top floor of the Security Pacific headquarters. Additionally, present were representatives from the Federal Reserve and the FDIC. This would apparently be our last encounter with this group. Notwithstanding our poor history, I was naively optimistic about the tone of this meeting, knowing that they had gotten some retribution for our bad behavior during many encounters over the past few months. I arrived with my management team choreographed to offer them an elaborate and optimistic presentation. We planned to describe how we'd worked to mitigate our problem assets prior to becoming part of Bank of America, and how the merger would effectively end any questions regarding our capital levels and financial health.

I mistakenly joked before the meeting that I felt confident they would congratulate us on the merger and tell us we had done a good job, but perhaps, not offer flower bouquets.

Hearty congratulations were not what the lead examiner had on his agenda. After a rather tepid salutation, the examiner started in with detectable delight. "There are several serious matters to discuss." I winced at those words. "As you know, the financial situation of the company is not exactly robust. Many areas are bad but, to begin, let us focus on the worst: Asset Quality continues to deteriorate to near historic levels and threatens to topple the bank. As of the end of the year, you had $1.5 billion of non-performing real estate loans alone and held another $1.6 billion in repossessed real estate."

Here we go again, I thought. They will just never give up.

We sat frozen in our seats as he adopted the harsh syntax of a Marine Corps drill instructor and railed against every aspect of our corporation. "Too much real estate underwriting. Inadequate credit administration. Too much emphasis on marketing, asset growth and loan origination. Asset deterioration is at historic levels, threatening your company's very viability. More and more loss exposure growing every week. Because of this ongoing and rising erosion, the assistance of the regulators has, for some time, been necessary. In response to all our calls and words over the past few years, however, you have been generally unresponsive."

I scoffed at the last comment.

He continued: "Poor, poor forecasting. Earning prospects are feeble. Liquidity could be a disaster. Limp credit culture. Employees are under strain." An ongoing staccato of criticism.

Of course, the staff is under strain, I thought.

"Poor morale."

No shit, I almost blurted.

"While your capital is just at the required minimum, it is inadequate to support your magnitude of risk."

"We know," I said. "That is, of course, the basic reason we decided on the merger."

"And a judicious decision it is indeed to merge."

I thanked him for that; it was the kindest sentiment I'd yet heard from this guy.

He seemed to eschew any further discussion of the merger or of what we had done to fix our situation and rapidly moved onto his real focus. "Let's talk about personal responsibility, accountability, and the role of management in this critical situation.

I was now sure we would not be making any presentation.

"Wait a second," I said. "Where are we going here? Why are we discussing blame at this point? Last week you heard the results of the Board of Director's engaged special study you requested. And they said this entire issue of accountability is a straw man, a red herring. Why won't you listen to the results of your own study?"

He scoffed. "They employed consultants, and I can get consultants to say anything I want them to say."

"Then what was the purpose of the study?"

"To explain what happened. Cause and effect." he continued.

"Now we turn to you, Mr. Smith, the Chief Executive Officer." My staff's ears perked in amazement; he was going to dress down their boss. "It would seem you are largely accountable for this convulsion of falling dominos. Considering that conclusion, it would seem that you should not be considered the heir-apparent at Bank of America. That would seem to be out of the question."

Good God, I thought. This guy had already made me aware of that along with Rosenberg. He just wanted to add an exclamation point for my staff and was giving me a performance evaluation right here in front of my management team. What an asshole.

"Hold on a second. I had no idea the purpose of this review was to assign personal blame and provide career counseling. Even so, I never said I wanted to run Bank of America or that the new board would even want me to do so, notwithstanding its inclusion in our agreement. That decision is three or four years away and you have already made that point to me. And frankly, you're jumping to a lot of conclusions that I don't believe are substantiated by the facts.

"Furthermore, I remind you again that we chartered a special Board of Director's study committee, augmented by outside experts, to determine what exactly caused our problems and to find what, if any, personal fault current management bore for the decline of Security Pacific. You specifically asked for this study, and its findings are unambiguous. You and I both know that while the committee indicated several problem areas, the report falls far, far short of a lynch mob conclusion about current management." In fact, it had absolved management of direct blame.

"Finally, while I am always ultimately responsible and stand accountable for the institution, your conclusions cover a long period of time, far exceeding the six-month parameters of your exam. And your conclusions fail to recognize the significant accomplishments of the past two years. You are holding current management, and me, responsible for all the errors made, and excluding us from the achievements."

"Achievements?"

"Well, I think we've done a pretty good job. To refresh your memory, I noted facetiously, "we just sold our company to a larger company out of the north; we've solved the problem of capital and poor credit and, as a result, you have nothing more to be concerned about. I really don't understand the purpose of this meeting and your critical comments."

"Yes, to be sure, the merger is the deal of the century."

"I mean, please be fair about this. We take responsibility for our problems, but we have also prevented an economic catastrophe and saved your regulatory body from a significant amount of grief."

"Be that as it may, your institution's serious deterioration continues unabated. The quality of the asset portfolio is deteriorating. The capital level is deteriorating."

What was his point of this vituperation? I wondered. We'd solved the problem.

"Now let's specifically discuss management," He continued. This was getting grim. "Individually, while you may be entrepreneurs, collectively you are an inferior bunch. As for you, Mr. Smith, your leadership is lacking. There appears to be no disciplined credit culture. Your directors have not held management appropriately accountable. You have ignored repeated regulatory warnings, as if they are of little apparent consequence, and this has contributed to a malaise of arrogance."

"Whoa, wait. Hold on a second. I agree that earlier there were instances of arrogance on the part of many bankers in the way they treated regulators, but I don't think that has been true in these recent periods. You say that current management is, and I specifically am unsatisfactory? Why is management unsatisfactory?"

He reserved his harshest castigation for me. "Ultimately, you are accountable and bear the responsibility for this incipient decay."

ACCOUNTABLE – A business leader's willingness to assume accountability for the company's difficulties is important, but consideration of the circumstances should be included in any external effort to impugn management.

PATIENT – During stressful and difficult situations it is important for business leaders to maintain focus on the end results and to remain calm and patient.

I groped for words. "I accept accountability as the bank's Chairman and CEO. But I think we've faced our problems head on. We've taken your advice seriously, and we've behaved professionally and civilly, even when we felt your treatment was unreasonably harsh. We have not been reactive; we've been proactive wherever it makes sense to do so. We've drastically increased our oversight of criticized loans, we've set aside greater and greater levels of reserves, and we worked continually to develop better and more thorough safeguards and procedures to improve credit quality. We are doing everything humanly possible within the limits of the law to stabilize the health of our institution. We are even going to merge with a larger, healthier institution. I mean, what more could we possibly do? And why is management unsatisfactory? Give me one example."

"Okay, take this situation. Look at one of your former executive's vituperative remarks in your presence against a female regulator whom he called a 'bitch.' This is the type of thing. And you were there, heard it, and did nothing about it."

Was that the best he could come up with? — a three-year-old indiscretion by an employee who had subsequently been fired?

"That was unfortunate, and it should indicate to you why he was considered lacking in certain areas and eventually let go. But you still haven't told me why management is unsatisfactory, or why I'm unsatisfactory."

"Well," he said, "you are a very arrogant group, and you are a very arrogant person."

I absolutely couldn't believe my ears. "Now I can neither refute nor attest to the institution's arrogance, but I've never thought of myself as being an arrogant person."

"Well, you, you." His eyes skimmed the faces across the conference table. "You've all been very arrogant toward the regulators over the past many years. In one particularly egregious circumstance you went so far as to have a regulator removed because you disputed his findings."

A-ha, there it was again: Our former CEO's abuse of the regulators a half-decade ago was being revisited and dumped upon us now. It was payback time.

"You know we don't need to personalize this. For the past two years we've worked day and night like professionals to fix the problems, not to fix the blame. The origin of many of these problems goes back quite a way, and —"

"But, with all due respect, you may not have been the Chairman and CEO at the time, but you were certainly in the room when the decisions were made to grant these very pitiful real estate loans."

"First, when the decisions were made to originate these loans, we didn't think they were bad; otherwise we wouldn't have granted them in the first place. Second, these loans weren't bad until Congress passed a provision in FIRREA that created a new basis of valuation, mandating that we value properties at a fraction of what we imagined they might ultimately be worth. When we made these loans, how were we to know that the government was going to change the valuation process a few years down the line and force the short-term valuation of long-term properties securing the loans? Third, while yes, I attended many of these earlier meetings, I must tell you that I agreed entirely with the strategy of making these loans. And finally, I can tell you with certainty that had I disagreed with those strategies, I wouldn't be sitting here so enjoyably in this room listening to your 'get even' comments, because our CEO would have fired me."

He snickered.

"Yes, I was in the room, and I'm proud I was in the room; it was my job to be in the room. And, for the most part, I thought we made the right decisions at the time. And the last time I checked, Security Pacific Corporation, our holding company, was still rated as a satisfactory organization."

"Not anymore. The Federal Reserve now considers the holding company unsatisfactory." "Your board will soon be made aware of this. Accordingly, and considering my comments, the overall condition of Security Pacific Bank is also now unsatisfactory."

It was a humiliating moment for me, and the end for Security Pacific. I was kidding myself to think there would be some regulatory flicker of appreciation or acknowledgment; there would be no warm phone calls, thank-you notes, or bouquets. They would continue to pummel the stuffing out of us, right to the bitter end.

The lead examiner had made his points and closed the books on our ongoing battles. Our management had lost in this conflict, as had I. But it was, interestingly, only six months later that this same lead examiner left his regulatory responsibilities to become an Executive Vice President at the new Bank of America. I later wondered if the "fix" was in.

BANK OF AMERICA REJECTS US

While the regulators were routinely having their moment in the sun by gaining a sense of revenge for our bad social behavior during the past decade, the top-level Bank of America staff was seeking control of their future in a purge conducted by their loyalists, all at the expense of our key staff. Their purge started early and was growing as the deal was nearing finalization.

They had initially refused to keep a few of our key senior personnel because they had been former Bank of America employees who had left to seek greater opportunities. Now they were regularly rejecting any organizational or policy thought we might express to them. At first, we argued and sought collaborative decisions that would satisfy all our needs and work to build the strength and potential of the soon to be combined companies. We had agreed that in all situations we would select the best person for a job whether it was one of ours or one of theirs.

As the months and weeks passed leading up to the final merging of our companies, however, their willingness to compromise or accept any of our ideas waned. Their rejection continued to the point that most of the thoughts and ideas of our senior officers, who would assume positions in the new company, were overlooked. It became apparent that they were winning the battle for control and dominance of the surviving company and that we were expected to feel lucky that we were being included and considered at all. They had become the alpha male.

Personnel selections for unit, group, or branch combinations were not shared but were becoming primarily Bank of America staff with Security Pacific personnel used for fillers. They had decided, with some vague explanations, that our Southern California headquarters tower would be abandoned in favor of their office complex, even though our location was considered superior and a major recognizable building. The new board committees were dominated and favored by their board members serving as the chairs. We were losing, and they were winning, in part because of their stronger financial position and the whispering and consent of the regulators on important decisions. We were also being encouraged by both Bank of America and the regulators to accelerate our loan write-downs so that the losses would be reported in our results and not in those of the new Bank of America following the merger.

As our problems magnified and the fulfillment of the merger agreement became questionable at times, it also became obvious to me that arguing or making an issue of our disagreements was not in our best interests. Our primary objective and the obvious necessary actions for all our constituents and especially the investor shareholders were that we do whatever was required to finalize the transaction and to not give Bank of America any reason to attempt to find a way out.

Early on, I had called a meeting of my senior staff to make sure we were all on the same page as we progressed to combine the two companies. I explained my view of the situation and told them that it was always appropriate and honest to express their feelings and thoughts on matters related to the merger. However, I wanted no serious disputes or battles if Bank of America seriously contested or debated our thoughts. I suggested that in such situations they should maintain their views but ultimately agree with the Bank of America position. In this way, we would recognize that they would win, however, I did not want the Bank of America staff to have any reason to challenge the fulfillment of the merger agreement.

ETHICAL – Under many circumstances, business leaders can be considered honest and ethical without fully conveying the full fact basis for decisions or actions to the other party. An insular response can be expressed in order to fulfill a larger, more significant objective.

A few weeks before the intended merger date I was told by Rosenberg that even though I would be the combined companies' President and Chief Operating Officer following the merger, I would only be expected to be involved in and report on the actions of Southern California charities and community issues. He noted that this action was a move that was aggressively supported by the regulators. He said he expected that all banking and operating matters and decisions be passed to him or his staff for consideration. It was obvious that while I was officially part of the company's management and its board, I was being stripped of any authority. I was cut out of any decision-making capacity. They didn't want me around, and along with the regulators had played me to the end. But the end was my goal; the combining of our companies, the added capital, increasing stock prices, and opportunities for our employees and definitely not what position or role or position I might hold.

17

SURVIVAL

THE SHAREHOLDERS APPROVE THE "MURDER"

The final shareholder approval of the merger was scheduled to take place about thirty days before the expected closing and even before the uncertain ERISA matter was resolved. I continued on the yet unsubstantiated idea that we would be able to solve this painful issue. Our shareholder meetings had traditionally been attended by a large group of our retirees, and I was sure that this meeting would be no exception. I expected a strong retiree attendance in view of the difficulties we had experienced and what appeared to be the dominant positions assigned to the Bank of America personnel. In addition, many of the retirees were emotionally involved in the company as shareholders or had spent their entire careers with the company. Others remained unhappy after witnessing, with deep concern, the passing of the leadership torch to me. This group felt that I had put the company at risk by pursuing the Merchant Bank strategy rather than focusing on building our basic branch banking business.

I wanted the retirees to feel welcome and to express their feelings and pour out their hearts regarding our troubles, the merger, and the historical meaning of the bank. But I knew the media would undoubtedly cover the official shareholder meeting, and I didn't want this important event to degenerate into a spectacle of negative thoughts. This was a concern because the retiree group had a propensity to have too many cocktails as they awaited the start of these shareholder meetings. The consumption of too many drinks often opened them to enjoy free-flowing but often negative expressions about management, the past and the expected future. I wanted any questions or comments from the floor to be normal or helpful to the merger transaction and to avoid any confusion or irrational outbursts.

For this reason, we arranged to have a special pre-shareholders meeting, exclusively for the retirees on the day prior to the official meeting. The retiree cocktail hour and luncheon would be held at the Bonaventure Hotel in downtown Los Angeles, which was the same venue scheduled for the shareholders meeting.

Meticulously orchestrated as both an opportunity for free expression and as a dress rehearsal, the format and business was to be the same as the following day's official shareholder meeting.

The retirees began to trickle in to the hotel convention area for the noon luncheon and meeting around 10:30 a.m., availing themselves of the open bar. These early arrivers did not hesitate to order their usual martinis, manhattans, and bloody mary drinks. This luncheon would break the Bonaventure's house record for the most liquor consumed at any noon function. Free liquor proved to be a significant attraction to this group of about 1500 former employees, spouses, and a few other relatives and friends, many of whom were also shareholders.

During lunch, the cocktails continued for many attendees, and as expected, the meeting portion became exceedingly emotional.

In the style of an open-mike night at City Hall, and following the formal presentation, retiree after retiree poured out their hearts in the Q and A session.

Sentimentality was evident and operating on all cylinders in the form of memories, poignant stories, bank-haiku, poems, and recollections.

Included were kind words about former bank leaders. Some of them even resurrected remembrances from the Great Depression. The meeting took on the aura of a memorial service as the eulogies continued. Many of the retirees spoke with a power and passion that nearly brought tears to my eyes. Some felt that with the passing of the Security Pacific name, their own history would pass as well. The issue was very personal. Very few of them were sympathetic to the merger, even though they would financially benefit if they owned our stock. It didn't matter to them that investor shareholders were the first priority in the thought process leading to the merger. Many didn't care about the good exchange ratio or the insured dividends; to some of them, it was as if an old friend had passed away.

Some retirees were complimentary, while others were heartbroken and choked with emotion: "My company is going away; my bank is going away; my friends are going away. I think they are taking over and we won't have as much say in our future. This just won't be the same company. I know it won't be."

Some of them funneled their upset into single issues that had enormous symbolic value for them:

"When they send me my retirement check, will it still say, 'Security Pacific' on it?"

"I think the merger is the best solution to the problem, but I don't want the Security Pacific name to go away. Can't the company keep its name?"

"I don't care if it's a good deal. What I care about is Security Pacific; my pride in this bank, this particular name. By the way, will the new organization — I refuse to call it Bank of America — have a Retiree's Club?"

I assured them that we would have a retiree's club going forward and tried my best to sound enthusiastic when I told them, "Now you'll be part of the Bank of America Retirees Club."

"I don't want to be part of the Bank of America Retirees Club. I want to be part of the Security Pacific Retirees Club."

No matter how much detail I went into, how meticulously I took them through the thought process that had led to the merger, I could not alter their unhappiness.

"I know Security Pacific has had a rough year, but are things so bad we have to resort to this?"

By the end of the luncheon, I was emotionally drenched in regret. I felt like crawling out of the Bonaventure Hotel.

––––––––––––––

The official shareholder meeting was serious but nowhere near as gut-wrenching as the retiree luncheon. There were fewer in attendance than we'd anticipated; many proxies had already been received by mail. The meeting, though tense, was productive.

I felt good about the meeting because in our collective leadership, even with considerable difficulties and problems, we had met the investor shareholder expectations. The stock price was twenty dollars per share when the deal with Bank of America was signed. We had expectations of the share price falling to single digits by the end of the year without a saving deal; or if the current merger happened to fail, we could see the share price dropping to four dollars. The stock price outlook of the deal as forecast by the security analysts was strong. They saw the earnings outlook and shareholder value gain of the merger to be significant.

> FINANCIAL UNDERSTANDING – *Understanding how the company's value is determined and the impact expense reductions and growth strategies have on the anticipated company value are important to business leadership.*

I opened the shareholder's meeting by asking those present to pause for a moment in the memory of the passing of our former CEO. "He served you, the shareholders, for thirty-seven- years, the last eleven of which were as the Chairman of the Board. His accomplishments over this period provided the foundation for this proposed murder with Bank of America."

I didn't realize I'd misspoken until the entire audience broke up in hysterical laughter.

I inserted an unscripted line: "Yikes, Well, I guess that's what many of you were thinking anyway." This embarrassing misstatement had a salutary effect; the tense atmosphere was suddenly broken, and my opening monologue and the meeting proceeded without a glitch.

I introduced and thanked key executives and several people who'd been instrumental in the merger negotiations.

In the first moments of my speech I reflected on the history of Security Pacific. "Without previous mergers, acquisitions, and consolidations, Security Pacific would not be what it is today." I took them back to April 10, 1871, when Isaias Hellman opened his safe to a Los Angeles of only seven thousand residents. I retraced our founder's ascent and Security Bank's expansion, took shareholders through the logarithmic growth of the corporation's assets, and brought them up to the important decision they had to make today. "This historic step surpasses the dreams, ideals, and expectations of all previous directors and the six leaders who preceded me and directed our company through so many challenges and changes."

Optimistically, I added, "Let me assure you that the spirit and history of Security Pacific is far from over. Each of the many smaller and several larger banks that helped Security Pacific become the fifth largest bank holding company in the United States lives within the fabric of our company. The legacy of our founders and the company's many leaders continues. Our history does not disappear. It becomes part of the new Bank of America, where our two histories and cultures merge to live on in a new greatness."

I summarized the events of the late decade, describing the regulatory environment, new laws and regulations such as FIRREA, the sluggish economy, the credit crunch, the absence of banking reform, and the appearance of unforeseen competition. I took shareholders through the process that led to the merger and emphasized the impact a sliding economy would continue to have on the corporation unless we pursued this option with haste. I talked about the overcapacity of the banking market and the partial answer to be found in consolidation.

What I purposely didn't discuss was that we anticipated we would reduce our combined staffs by 10 to 15% or 12,000 to 18,000 persons, knowing that this adjustment would add significantly to the company's expected earnings. I also didn't discuss that several key executives would lose their positions or that I expected that our customers would not be as well served by the new bank, which would be employing Bank of America's less friendly and more controlling policies. Left out, in addition, was that the new combined bank would offer less support to the community's charitable entities, many of which served lower income neighborhoods.

As I proceeded, I took shareholders through the exchange ratio and stock conversion process. "The board of directors of Security Pacific believe the merger is in the best interests of Security Pacific and its investor shareholders and unanimously recommends that you vote for the approval and adoption of the agreement."

I opened the floor to questions pertaining to the merger.

The questions were germane and on point. There were no tears, no speeches, no strolls down Memory Lane, and no snockered retirees.

In response to an angry query about the recent suspension of the dividend, I said, "I recognize that the suspension of our common stock dividend is especially painful to shareholders who depend on it for income, and I would just implore you to consider the uncertainty of our economic future and our need to maximize corporate strength, especially now."

I expressed the hope that I would not have to "pull" my parachute that personally financially protected me from disfavor with the Bank of America management. On the contrary, I felt a duty to stick with the combined company and would do so if there was a meaningful role for me to assume in the merged organization. Why would any banker in his right mind turn down an opportunity to help run what would be the largest and most powerful bank in the United States? A somewhat naïve response to the broad range of criticism received from the regulatory community and the growing negative expressions of Bank of America executives.

ETHICAL– Carefully crafting answers to difficult questions yet remaining ethical and truthful is an important quality of successful and responsible business leaders.

After the Q&A, we handed out ballots. We adjourned the meeting for ten minutes while a final vote was counted and verified. When we reconvened, the secretary reported on the results of the vote.

Shareholders approved the merger by an overwhelming 98% voting in favor of the transaction.

In the end, most of our expectations were justified because in the months following the deal closing, the value for Security Pacific shareholders was approaching forty dollars per share. We had successfully fulfilled this important objective for the investor shareholders and struggled hard, with only limited success, to protect the interests of most employees without jeopardizing the deal. I wasn't sure that too many of our customers were particularly happy with Bank of America policies and the dearth of communications when compared to the service we had offered.

Over the early period leading up to this event, the leaders of Bank of America had chosen to lead us on with generally good solutions to ongoing issues, particularly some of the early personnel decisions. In the more recent period, however, we discovered that many of their promises were false, misleading, and full of untruths. They had, to some degree, played us all to close the deal while maintaining their complete control.

WATCHING THE RIOTS WITH A GRIN

The pieces had at last fallen into place. I was thrilled to have been an important part of bringing together our failing "sick puppy" with a strong capital heavy bank that had the capacity to support our problem loans and preserve the market value of our investor shareholders. It had freed me from the nine month period of uncertainty; never being sure that this historic event would ever happen. In addition, I was free of the continuing regulatory denigration or of subjecting myself to personal board termination in an effort to preserve the company in the event that the deal had not closed or was seriously delayed.

I intended to stay on as the COO and as a director of Bank of America in order to preserve the interests of our thousands of employees but, considering their recent actions, I already had serious doubts if that would work. Following the first week together with the Bank of America executives and Dick Rosenberg, they wasted no time in confirming for me through their words and actions that I had no meaningful role to play in the combined companies or much to add to the ongoing success of the Bank of America.

After that first week, I made up my mind that I would leave the company as soon as possible. I already had a very bad taste in my mouth and concern about the impact their superior attitude and controlling nature would have on our employees, customers, and the communities, notwithstanding the positive impact that this transaction had for our investor shareholders. I would leave the new Bank of America within six months. Contrary to my hope expressed at the final shareholders' meeting, I would pull my parachute. When I informed Rosenberg of my decision, I made it very clear that he or his management committee would never hear me report, as he had suggested, on the Red Cross or other charitable groups from Southern California. I facetiously noted for his sake that I felt this was below my expectations and pay grade.

It was seven days following the completion of the tenth largest mergers in U.S. history that I had a most reflective moment of thought. Standing in my office on the 54th floor of our headquarters building overlooking the entire Los Angeles area, I was witnessing a much bigger event taking place. An activity that could impact our new combined companies, including its employees, customers, and the many citizens in our communities.

The city was in chaos and in many places on fire. The citywide rioting was the result of the Rodney King jury decision that found four white L.A. Police officers not guilty of the beating of Mr. King during his arrest in South-Central Los Angeles.

As I looked out of my corner windows at the fury of a city in turmoil I saw that the chaos was well under way with uncontrolled looting, fighting, arson, and the destruction of personal property.

Three dozen columns of smoke were streaming up into the sky, some in areas within a few blocks of downtown Los Angeles. Others were evident on the horizon going South and West of the downtown area. I was unhappy and sad about the impact this would have on our city and its many residents, yet I grinned just a bit knowing that had this event occurred a couple of weeks prior, it most likely would have severely impacted the completion of our merger.

I was, for that moment, extremely pleased with what had been accomplished. I was proud of the team that had worked so hard to successfully reach a positive ending. On the other hand, I was saddened that while we had sought to fairly balance the interests of all those who, for decades, had been part of our bank, many had fared better than others. Some were pleased, and others were saddened by the end of the one-hundred-twenty-year history of Security Pacific.

As it turned out, the history of Security Pacific did not live on as I had so proudly noted at the approving shareholder's meeting. Neither, however, did Bank of America and most of its leadership team, as six years later, employing the same alpha male style, Nations Bank merged with Bank of America. Nation's Bank took control of the board of directors, abated a succession provision of the merger agreement, and moved the headquarters to Charlotte, North Carolina in another merger deal that ended up like ours; one-sided and on a somewhat sour note.

ADDENDUM

SIGNIFICANT LEADERSHIP QUALITIES

I ndividual personal leadership attributes are a combination of inherent and developed qualities. These essential traits, consistently exercised, are identified as primary to the leader's ability to be effective and to successfully manage and lead an organization. These qualities include the four primary aspects of the best executives, owners, managers, and bosses: a preferred leader profile; desirable personal behavioral characteristics; specific personal value characteristics and necessary operational skills.

PREFERRED LEADER PROFILE

Business leaders at all levels develop a personal profile that includes elements of specific knowledge that can be routinely applied in the performance of their responsibilities. Most of these are developed through formal education in multiple disciplines and specialties or are advanced through relevant and applicable experience in specific areas.

POSSESS A STONG UNDERSTANDING OF FINANCIAL ISSUES (FINANCIAL UNDERSTANDING)

The best business leaders have an extensive knowledge of finance, accounting, investment, and taxes, both from their rules and principles to their impact on real and contemplated decisions, actions, and transactions. An understanding of the financial impact in terms of the expected results and risks to the company can affect the viability, strength, and potential of the entity. It is difficult to make sound decisions without a strong understanding of all financial issues.

KNOWLEDGE OF HOW THE ECONOMY IMPACTS DECISIONS (ECONOMIC KNOWLEDGE)

Understanding the impact of economic history, change, and expectations on all decisions and actions of the company is an important quality for effective leadership at most business levels. The ability to evaluate and anticipate local, national, and world economic change and its impact on companies, industries, and individuals is an important skill for successful leaders.

DEMONSTATE A KEEN AWARENESS OF LEGAL MATTERS (LEGAL AWARENESS)

Gaining a relevant background and knowledge of the legal and regulatory issues and their potential impact on decisions and actions of the company are essential for successful business leaders. While professional legal assistance is always available and should be used as necessary, the ability to have a personal understanding of legal and regulatory matters is an important element in leadership.

UNDERSTANDS INDUSTRY PRACTICES AND BUSINESS STANDARDS (UNDERSTAND PRACTICES AND STANDARDS)

Having a thorough knowledge of industry practices and standards, including regulatory expectations, is an important trait required of effective business leaders. A leader's ability to effectively structure the company's policies and actions while considering the traditional, formal, and informal rules and policies as well as industry standards and expectations is an important element in the company's success.

DESIRABLE PERSONAL BEHAVIORAL CHARACTERISTICS

Successful business leaders carry both developed and inherent personal behavioral characteristics as necessary elements to their effectiveness and performance in directing the many aspects that define a company. These personal characteristics are evident in the thoughts, expressions, and actions of the leader in managing and directing the company. Each of the areas identified and discussed are important to the effectiveness and ability of the leader to fulfill the expectations and mission of the organization. These areas are all necessary to collectively satisfy the needs of the investor shareholders, customers, employees, and the broader communities.

COMMITTED TO THE COMPANY (COMMITTED)

It is essential for business leaders to be passionate and fully committed to the company's mission and the actions necessary to fulfill its expectations. In addition, it is important that leaders are committed to exercise all the personal qualities required to effectively exercise good leadership and resolve specific matters. Any failure to orally and visibly express passion and commitment to the company and its mission can be detrimental to the performance of the leader and the company.

EXHIBITS POSITIVE CONFIDENCE (CONFIDENT)

One of the more significant qualities of effective business leaders is the ability to approach situations and actions with positive thinking and confidence. This is most essential during times of distress, uncertainty, or trouble. All individuals and affiliate groups that can influence the company look to the leader to understand the situation and to gain confidence in the intended outcome.

ACTS DECISIVELY IN RESOLVING MATTERS (DECISIVE)

The ability for business leader to resolve any uncertain or unclear issues with decisive action is essential to maintaining the support and confidence of all individual and affiliate groups. The ability to be decisive in seizing sound opportunities while directing both a patient and disciplined organized process without becoming either contemplative or uncertain is a strong attribute of a good leader.

UNDERTAKES ACTION WITHOUT FEAR (FEARLESS)

Decisions and action should be expressed and undertaken without fear. This is best accomplished by gathering, discussing, and debating all available information to arrive at decisions that minimize any fear of the expected outcome. The best business leader cannot exhibit fear in executing the necessary actions; otherwise individuals and affiliate groups will become cautious or suspicious of the value of the decision or hesitant in its execution. Actions taken under troubled circumstances, even with uncertainties, cannot change the necessity of the leader's ability to avoid any expressions that convey fear.

EXERCISES A DISCIPLINED DECISION PROCESS (DISCIPLINED)

Business leaders should be disciplined and predictable in exercising their leadership. Managing executive decisions with a consistent process and in a disciplined format is an essential ingredient in good management. This process combines consideration of all aspects of the business mission, objectives, and individual strategies. It also considers the financial implications, social mission of the company, and the possible uncertainties and risks to the organization.

RESPONDS WITH PATIENCE (PATIENT)

It is often important for business leaders to respond to issues with a quick decision. In most situations, however, it is a better choice for leaders to act with a patient and calm demeanor and to think through the matter before initiating a response. This includes identifying the issues and gathering the relevant information, including listening to others, considering alternative action, and responding with a well thought through decision and action plan. Acting too quickly without a thorough process for decision making will often produce less effective results than utilizing a patient process. In addition, remaining patient generally removes impact of personal or group emotion from the decision-making process of the company, and the possible uncertainties and risks to the organization.

SPECIFIC PERSONAL VALUE CHARACTERISTICS

Success in business leadership requires that those in charge have a value composition that insures they act and make decisions that will withstand time and the review of others. A good element of a leader's success is dependent on their ability to sustain positive views and opinions of all those whom they touch and affect each day.

EXERCISES FAIRNESS IN DECISION MAKING (FAIR)

The ability for business leaders to act with fairness to all interests is an essential ingredient to the success of the company. Acting fairly is necessary to maintain the support and respect of all related parties and groups. Fairness is generally determined by the willingness to listen to each position and to weigh and reason the arguments against the broader objectives and principles of the company. Matters that are considered generally fair are more easily reasoned and accepted by the staff and related groups. It is important that leaders believe they have acted fairly and equitably in their decision making.

CONVEYS COMPASSION (COMPASSIONATE)

Many issues go beyond just the facts and have a personal impact on others within or outside the organization. It is important for business leaders to consider the need for compassion and understanding of matters that can impact persons unfairly. Most significantly, showing compassion establishes a leader's relationship with all involved with the company. Pursuing relationships with the understanding of other difficulties or concerns in a constructive, warm, congenial way sets a tone for working together to obtain mutual objectives.

ASSUMES ACCOUNTABILITY (ACCOUNTABLE)

Respected business leaders should be willing to assume the accountability for all the positives but also the decisions and actions that fail to meet the objectives of the company. It is generally wrong for a leader to blame other individuals or circumstances for failed strategies or missed results. Whether the error was in the strategy, tactic, structure, or execution, good leaders are expected to assume accountability for the results.

ACTS WITH HIGH ETHICAL VALUES (ETHICAL)

The expression of ethical values including honesty and truthfulness, is a basic element of business leaders and is often a determinant of their credibility. It is impossible to gain support or respect as a leader if the incumbent is, in fact or perceived to be, an untruthful or unethical person. Living up to one's word or commitment and not distorting matters for financial or personal gain are essential ingredients of these values. When a leader is confronted with questions that could negatively impact individuals or the company if answered directly, it is often acceptable to avoid transparency by not recognizing or directly responding to the question.

NECESSARY OPERATIONAL SKILLS

Elements of a business leader's operational leadership skills are matters that can be gained through both formal education and periods of experience. These areas have elements of developed style and factors of process discipline consistent with the company's mission and expectations.

EFFECTIVELY COMMUNICATES WITH FOCUSED CONSISTENCY (COMMUNICATIVE)

The ability of a business leader to deliver organized and consistent oral and written communications that send a clear direction or message to staff and affiliates is critical to good leadership. Communications should be focused and effectively delivered so that the recipients gain a full clear understanding of all aspects of decisions, including intended change, required action, or priorities.

COMMITED TO LISTENING AND
CONSIDERING VIEWS OF OTHERS (COLLABORATIVE)

Good business leaders are dependent on strong communicative qualities, but it is equally essential that they are strong listeners of the views and opinions of all. Their decisions should be inclusive of all voices, gaining the perspective of staff, employees, customers, and affiliate groups. Collaboration is essential to good decision making and to maintaining the support of all impacted parties. The willingness to bring together the interests of the parties is essential to gain the support of decisions that impact all aspects of the organization.

REMAINS ORGANIZED IN ADDRESSING ISSUES (ORGANIZED)

A business leader should address issues, changes, and processes in an organized manner. Applying a structured process that leads to full consideration of the relevant matters is critical to an organized resolution of issues. Disorganization leads to poor decisions, omissions of relevant information, and poorly structured responses.

CAPABLE OF DETERMINING AND EVALUATING RISK (PROTECTIVE)

The business leader should provide a protective environment of the risks associated with decisions and matters to be considered. This requires a full understanding and evaluation of transactions and decisions, considering the related environment, economy, industry, financial factors, and all related implications. Such decisions should be made while considering the value or potential benefits as compared with the exposure to risk associated with the decisions.

SKILLED AT DEVELOPING OPPORTUNITIES
AND MARKETING STRATEGIES (CREATIVE)

Strong business leaders should be creative, entrepreneurial, and aware of the need and opportunity to establish new or expand existing products, services, and business combinations that can build the market reach of the customer base. This skill includes understanding contemporary marketing strategies and techniques that can enhance the ability to achieve strong financial results.

EFFECTIVE AT JUDGING PEOPLE (SELECTIVE)

Business leaders are responsible for the formation of their staff. A principal responsibility of leaders is to determine, organize, and select those who are expected to and can excel at performing their responsibilities. Leaders should be skilled at identifying the qualities and characteristics necessary for effectively filling important positions. They should also be able to fairly and rationally select the best and most qualified persons for all leadership positions.